"Mill Road"

by Brian Jenkins

Every Welsh town had a Mill Road.
Every Mill Road had a Brian Jenkins.

Published 2008 by arima publishing

www.arimapublishing.com

ISBN 978 1 84549 292 2

Printed and bound in the United Kingdom

Typeset in Garamond 12/14

Swirl is an imprint of arima publishing.

arima publishing
ASK House, Northgate Avenue
Bury St Edmunds, Suffolk IP32 6BB
t: (+44) 01284 700321

www.arimapublishing.com

Acknowledgements

This book is dedicated to my good friend and neighbour of fifteen years, David Leighfield, who sadly died before I finished this book. After thousands of cups of his famous coffee and putting the world to right, his encouragement for me to carry on was immense. I shall never forget him.

I thank my niece Melissa, my son Jonathan and his wife Debbie for helping me to improve my grammar and typing skills, and my wife Dianne for her patience and understanding.

Our three sons, Martyn, Richard and Jonathan, with their respect, have shown me how life can be a great adventure, while exquisite moments with my grandchildren have helped me recall a small child's marvel.

I am privileged.

TO SHARON & NIAMH

BEST WISHES

UNCLE. Brian

30 · MARCH 2008.

I can remember....

I can remember when I was a lad
The name of each kid in our class.
I can say them off the tip of my tongue,
Every spotty young boy, every lass.

I remember the Boys Brigade
And a biscuit called Marie.
I still know the words of the songs we sang
On coach trips to Porthcawl and Barry.

I can remember in those days of fraught
The lessons we had every day.
I still know the poems and things we were taught
And the words of the school Christmas play.

I remember our divvy number from the co-op;
It was five nine six.
I remember bread units and ration books too
And paying a bob for the flicks.

I remember collecting jam jars for cash
And remember when sweets first came off ration.
I remember Ken Blake, Glyn Horler and Mike
And when a DA haircut was fashion.

How is it, seeing my memory's so good
And I recall all the girls' eyelashes,
Yet no matter how hard I rack my brain
I can't think where I put my glasses!

Chapters

Preface

Brian Jenkins was born in South Wales in 1940. Although he lived for a short time in Halifax during the war his home was Pontypool, South Wales. Living with his family in a gas board cottage with no electricity or a bathroom, sandwiched between a rubbish tip and a gasworks. The family struggled for many years with the ups and downs of life in South Wales.

When Brian was 18 the family moved to a new council house. Brian now lives in New Inn, Pontypool with his wife. His has three grown up boys and six grandchildren and is now retired.

Chapter 1

Goodbye Aunty Marge

Springtime, a time for looking forward, a time for new beginnings, new life and new journeys. This bright and sunny Sunday morning, I glanced from our bungalow, across at the impending green valley, a valley that has witnessed so many changes. Through winter, spring, summer and autumn, patterns are created over and over again. Today, early spring, bright, crisp and so inviting, the daffodils stand proud, taking over from the snowdrops that spread like a blanket over the hillside as winter says goodbye for now. Anytime now the lambs will appear, playful as ever and as white as the last snows of spring. My home, my valley, my breathtakingly beautiful eastern valley where I have run, played and frolicked as a child. So green and so full of life – how lucky we are to be surrounded by such natural beauty.

I heard the sound of a steam engine's whistle on the railway line a few hundred yards away, so I begin to walk to the railway bridge a few minutes walk from my home. As I looked over from the bridge I saw a magnificent looking Steam Engine with shiny black and green paintwork, pulling two immaculate red antique carriages just arriving at Pontypool's New Inn Halt. Now a barren strip of tarmac, with a glass shelter in the centre, and just a small bench to sit on inside. Shame really. In its day, it was a bustling place, full of excitement, anticipation and awe. Now, open and bleak, situated on the main line between South Wales and the north of Britain, two miles south of Pontypool, eight miles north of Newport;.

A crowd of people, full of praise for the train's excellent well-kept condition, had gathered to see the "Union of South Africa no 60009" steam engine on display, carrying out a special run between Shrewsbury and Cardiff for rail enthusiasts; it was such a thrill. They hurried around excitedly taking photos from all angles in pure admiration of this spectacular piece of machinery in front of them. The driver was a short plump-looking fellow with red cheeks and a welcoming smile. By his side stood the fireman, tall, thin and pale with a long beaky nose. They looked similar to the comedians Laurel and Hardy.

Soon enough the engine sounded its whistle and slowly pulled away to head south to Cardiff. In a bellowing cloud of steam, with driver and fireman waving farewell, she was gone from my valley. The crowd dispersed and headed to their cars in the nearby car park and all seemed happy and satisfied with the recent experience. I gazed over at the empty, silent, even ghost-like platform and slowly walked back home. With this scene in my head, my thoughts began to wander back, back to a time long gone, lost forever a time never to return again, but a time that will live forever in my memories. As I reach the garden at my home, my wife Dianne is there, welcoming me with a big smile and a cup of tea. I begin to talk about the scene I have witnessed and the pictures in my mind. "How things have changed in the last sixty years.

My mind drifted back to 1943 World War Two was still raging; I was three years old. 'Pontypool Road Station' as it was called then, was very large and had one of the longest platforms in the country. 'The Road' was still on the main line from South Wales to the North, but with many branch lines stretching in all directions. To the west it headed to the Vale of Neath via Crumlin Viaduct. Also, there was a line to Blaenavon and east to Monmouth. 'The Road' always seemed to be hidden in a cloud of steam and smut, bustling with trains, constantly coming and going, carrying coal from the valleys, and carrying passengers and goods to all parts of Britain. People would scurry between the booking office waiting rooms, to and from the Café, or Buffet as they called it back then. There were always soldiers around, standing at the bar drinking with their haversacks stood beside them; it was wartime after all. Pontypool had three stations; Crane Street, Clarence Street and by far the largest, Pontypool Road.

"Bye Aunty Bye Uncle George,' were the words that I can vividly remember saying. 'Bye Michael," See you all when we come home.'

Mam and I were taking their daughter (my cousin) Jean, with us back to Halifax by train to be with my father. Jean was very pretty with long, dark flowing hair and she was around three years older than me, whereas Michael and I were the same age. I always loved everyone in the Smith family, but especially Aunty Marge, Mam's sister, very dearly.

"Goodbye for now Brian, look after Mam and Jean," they shouted, making me feel grown-up. It was a cold, damp morning, typical Welsh weather, no sign of the winter sun on that day. We all stood at the platform in our overcoats and scarves to keep out the cold. Mam held Jean and me up to the window to kiss them goodbye. After the door had closed, the train pulled out of the station with Aunty, Uncle and cousin Michael waving goodbye to us.

My mother, Ursula Marion Jenkins, whose maiden name was Jones, was born on Christmas day 1916. Born into a large family of fifteen, there were 10 girls and 5 boys. She was the eighth born after Aunty Marge. The family lived at a place called Cwmffrwdoer which was around two miles north of Pontypool. Home was a modest three bedroom terrace property with no bathroom, a small front and rear garden with six small steps leading up to the front door. I don't know how they all lived there, but they managed somehow. As one was coming into the world, another was leaving home to get married. Two of the eldest, Millie and Olwyn, married and left home to live in London. Phyllis, Floss and Marge had also flown the nest but lived nearby. Alf, Albert and Jack were abroad serving in the Navy while Billy served in the Air Force. Kathleen, Dolly, Esme, Gwyneth and Derek were still at home.

In 1896, my grandfather James "Checky" Jones departed from Liverpool aboard the RMS Teutonic for America and landed at Ellis Island, New York on November 29. He went to work in the coal mines of Pittsburgh Pennsylvania, but through homesickness he returned home four years later to Wales and married my grandmother Carrie Rogers. Sadly, she died before I was born. Her life must have been a hard one but full of the joys and heartaches of family life; nurturing and encouraging her babies and watching her children grow. Granddad Jones was a very pleasant man, short and plump with a round jolly looking face. He always wore a white shirt and black waistcoat with a long row of buttons up the front. He always sat in "his chair" in the corner of the front room. Hanging on the wall above his head was a picture of the ship that brought him home from America. To the left of this was a wall cupboard where he kept a large tin of sweets, ready to give to any grandchild that may come along to visit. "Got summit nice for you little un," he often said. 4 Pleasant View, Hanbury Road was a very apt address. Through the window could be seen a breathtaking view of a small mountain known locally as the "Tump". "Take me oop Tump, Granddad," I would plead every time I visited. "I can't today, Sunny Boy, I've got a bone in my leg" he would answer. He did take me a few times when the weather was warm and he felt strong enough. I cherished the short time I had with him.

We were returning to Yorkshire, we had stayed with my aunt Emily, dad's oldest sister. Her husband Eddie Rowland was serving abroad in the Army. They had two children, Margaret 6 and John 3. Later, we spent our teenage years together as great pals. They lived at 13 Park Terrace, Charles Ville, and

Pontnewynydd. This is where I was born on the 6th August 1940 as my mother and father had no home to call their own at the time. Times were hard and filled with fear as German planes flew through our skies attempting to drop their bombs on a local arms factory based at Usk just a few miles away. We would huddle together and hide under the "cooch" which was a large cupboard under the stairs, just in case a stray bomb fell onto the house as they did in some cases. I was told that a bomb had fallen just outside the Globe Hotel in Pontypool town centre but luckily it didn't cause too much damage. The hotel remains in business to this day.

Our journey to Yorkshire was to take us to the town of Halifax where my father William Aubrey Jenkins, worked as a capstan operator at a local Armstrong Sidley factory. Dad was one of seven children, 3 boys and 4 girls. Emily, Ted, Aubrey, Margaret, Joyce, Reece and Iris. The Jenkins family, except for Emily, lived on a new housing estate at The Woodlands, Penygarn, one mile up a steep hill above town. They moved there in 1937 from a large dilapidated house at the bottom of a road called Mill Road. Ted was serving in the army abroad while Reece worked in Coventry in a factory producing armaments.

Our home in Halifax was a "works cottage" set in a row of houses known as Lower Hope Street. It was very small and cramped with two bedrooms, one room downstairs, a little pantry for food and a tiny kitchen with a small gas cooker with two rings on top. There was a yard at the front of the property with an outside toilet to the right of the front door and a cold water tap to the left. There was a narrow pavement that led to a stone cobbled road which in turn led to houses opposite that were exactly the same in structure and appearance. Dad worked during the night at the factory, so Mam, Jean and I slept on our own. As darkness fell, the German planes came and air raid sirens would pierce all around and disturb our once contented sleep. We would cower underneath our thick, heavy blankets, clutching each other tightly, Mam saying "Don't worry, it will all be over soon and we can go back home to Wales." Jean and I never really got used to it, but we did manage to sleep through some of these unwanted episodes. It wasn't as easy for Mam as I knew she laid there awake and worrying about Dad working throughout the night and knowing that the Germans were targeting the aeroplane factories where he worked. In the morning, I would sit outside on a small coal bucket, turned upside down and wait for Dad to come home. "Daddy, Daddy," I would yell, as he came around the corner at the bottom of the street. Off the bucket I would jump and run down to greet him, diving up into his strong, welcoming arms. I loved my father so much. After breakfast, which was always tea and toast, I would go up to bed with him and curl up warm in his arms until we went to sleep. "Let's go to Shroggs Park, Mam" were the first words I usually said. "Okay, if it's not raining" was always her reply. I loved to go to places with Mam and Jean. Sometimes we would go to Huddersfield or Rochdale on the bus for the day, or shopping in Halifax town, which was walking distance away. My mother always looked for the cheapest goods to buy as we were really very poor. People would call us the little family from Wales. Just around the corner at the bottom of Lower Hope Street was a small shop that was run by a very large man with a white apron and a shiny bald head. He had a long grey beard and he practically filled the shop with his huge frame. One day, Mam peered through the window and went inside. She asked for four pasties for our supper. Her proud Welsh accent was strong and very different from the locals. He looked at her and was obviously quite confused so he asked my mother to point out what she would like. With a loud laugh he replied "we call them savoury ducks". We never forgot what they call pasties in Yorkshire!

So many years later, Mam relayed this story time and time again to her granddaughters and great granddaughter and they too found her stories of the "olden days" very entertaining, listening intently to her tales from another space in time Our stay here was quite a happy one as everyone was so kind to us.

Not long after we first arrived in Halifax, Dad received a telegram from Aunt Emily, informing him of the sad news that his mother had died of breast cancer. My grandmother was just fifty five years old and she was a real lady. The photographs I have seen showed a true natural beauty, and to die so young was a huge loss to my family. Dad left us and headed home to Wales to say a final farewell to his dearly loved mother.

Poor Dad, he looked so sad, dressed in his old brown suit and carrying an old worn suitcase. It must have been an unhappy and lonely journey home, and the dark, cold days of war must have made things seem even more desperate. Thankfully, he didn't leave us for long. He was back with us after a few days, with the news that the rest of the family were well and his father, George, was coping well.

The only toys I had to play with were a small red wooden train and two little trucks. A carpenter at the factory had kindly made them for Dad to give to me. I thought they were the most wonderful, precious gifts anyone could have. Along with a few lead soldiers, I played with my toys for hours and hours. Sadly, a few days before we were due to leave, I came into the house after playing in the street. "Where's your train and soldiers?" Jean yelled. "O dear, I've left them out in the street," I replied. "Quick, go and get them." We ran as fast as we could out of the house and into the street to find them. We searched and searched, but they were gone. A passer-by must have picked them up and ran off. I was so unhappy I cried until Dad came home from work. He reassured me and gave me a hug and said he would get me some new toys when we got home. I was desperately sad and so angry with myself for leaving my toys outside. I cherished that little train set and soldiers so much.

January 1945

9 Lower Hope Street
Halifax

Dear Marge and George

I hope you all keeping well. Jean is saying she would like to come home to you, and I think she is missing you. I guess she has been up here long enough; we are all becoming homesick and would like to return to Wales.

I have to tell you that I am going to have a baby soon, its due in April, and I would rather have it back home in Wales. I told Brian that he is having a brother or sister, but his answer was that he would rather have a puppy. Jean was more excited as she is having a new cousin. If we return to Wales, Aubrey said that he can get a job in the mines and work along with George. The problem is, as you know, we have not anywhere to live. Do you think that we could stay with you for a while, until we get a place of our own? I will bring Jean home in a week or two, so don't worry.

Hope to hear from you soon.

Your loving sister,
Ursula.

Aunty Marge returned my mother's letter and said we would be very welcome to stay until we had a place of our own. Mam and Dad sold what little furniture they had and packed all our belongings in some old trunk cases to go back to Wales. We went around seeing as many friends as we could to say our goodbyes, always ending in tears and squeezing the breath out of me as they wished us good luck. Dad said that they would return one day, but they never did. 45 years later I would make an emotional return to that town in the north.

The journey home seemed endless, changing trains at Birmingham, with Dad struggling with the trunk cases. We had to wait hours for our connection and thought we would never see Wales again. Our journey was filled with excitement and anticipation. We had been away from the Welsh valleys and our family for so long and we couldn't wait for the train to arrive. We pulled into Pontypool Road station in the middle of the night and slept in some cold hard chairs in the waiting room until it was morning. Dad gave some money to a parcel delivery driver who gave us a lift to Auntie's in his van. I remember my father saying that we were happy to be home to the driver, but the truth was that the future must have seemed very bleak. No home, very little money and a baby on the way. At least we were back in our home country and surrounded by our family.

Chapter 2

Thirteen Days

The Smiths, Aunty Marge, Uncle George, Cousins Jean and Michael lived in a small three-bed roomed house. 6 Trosnant Street was situated at the top end of Trosnant and only around 300 yards from the Pontypool town centre. It was an end of terrace property with a shared water tap between four houses, set at the side of a small yard with two outside toilets between them. The Trosnant and Mill Road area was an extremely poor and deprived part of Pontypool, but the houses were always kept spotlessly clean and the people were very kind and remained happy to help one another at all times.

Trosnant used to be the main road from Pontypool to Newport and the south. It was a long road that started high then sloped down only to rise again at the other end. At the top end, near the Clarence and town were two public houses, the Hanbury Arms and the Waterloo. The Kings Arms was situated at the bottom end. Two scrap merchant brothers lived nearby, each with their own yard, Billy and Henry Harris. Henry had the nickname "Bottle Harris". Real rag and bone men, they were. "Bottle" had three sons, Graham, Butch and Malcolm. I recall always going to Malcolm with my scrap metal as he always weighed my wheelbarrow as well as the scrap. A great character was Malcolm, who used to wear six heavy gold chains around his neck and a handful of gold coins filling his pocket, a real wheeler dealer boy, but always honest and fair.

Also 'down' Trosnant were many small houses and cottages, spreading in all directions. There was a 'bottle factory', which was not actually a factory at all, but a mountain of empty bottles, stacked in an ever-growing heap behind a long gypsy caravan. The owner would buy empty bottles from us. "How much you givus for this lot mister?" I'd say as the man opened his caravan door. He was so huge that he would struggle to get through the door. He was so fat he had difficulty moving around and he always wore the same thick brown sweater. Large round eyes stared at you under a greasy cloth cap and a huge chin hung over his collar. "Give ew a penny lad", he'd say, staring into my little wheelbarrow full of empty bottles that I had collected from knocking upon the local doors. "Tha'en much, mun. C'mon, mister, givus tuppence". "Nah, who d'ya think I am Rothschild. I'll give you a penny an that's all!" "OK then", I said as I walked to the pile of bottles and tipped my wheelbarrow up. He would struggle to get back into the van and hand over the money reluctantly. He would sit in his little window looking out to make sure I didn't take any of the bottles with me. I would never dare! As I walked up the pathway to the gate and back out onto the road, I would always hear him say "shut the bloody gate!" I don't know what he ever did with all those bottles, but I guess he must have made some money out of them. He also bought rabbit skins and old clothes and rags.

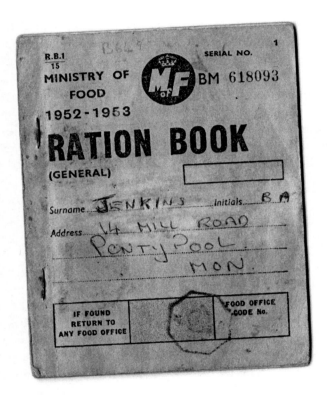

My Ration Book

There was also 'Young's Carpenters Shop', a few builders' yards and at the bottom end, just as the road joined the road to Newport, there was a blacksmith's shop. When the weather grew cold, the blacksmith would let you inside for a while for a warm up. "Pump up the bellows, lad! Keep the fire going" he would say.

The Kings Arms public house, owned by Sam James, could also be found at the bottom of Trosnant. It never closed and had long benches inside the corridor. Children would sit here waiting for their parents to come out. I remember peering inside the big dark room, full of smoke, climbing up to the low brown ceiling above. Smoke bellowed from the coal-fired round black stove that stood in the centre of the room, the chimney stack stood above it. When the wind blew hard back down the stack, the lid on top of the stove would lift and send smoke and flames shooting out like a fierce roaring dragon. Most of the men smoked pipes and cigarettes, or fags, as they called them. They were always 'pock faced' and still wearing the same clothes they had come home from the mines in. With their flat caps and dirty white scarves, they all looked just the same to me. The tables were covered in tobacco, fag ends and beer glasses. The ash and fag ends would be pushed onto the stone tiled floor; it was a proper spit 'n' sawdust pub. "Come on home, Dad. Mam's waitin' with yur grub", kids would shout in the doorway. "Won't be bloody long. Tell er, finishin me pint first" was the usual reply. Although times were hard and the families that lived near were poor, the men always seemed to have money to spend on drink.

Just up the road from the pub, a character named Algey lived. He was a fearsome looking man with a red face and a short black beard. He always wore a dirty black duffel coat, be it winter or summertime. He sat on a wooden chair outside his modest home and any stranger that walked by that he didn't like the look of would be shouted at. "Get back up Ponty this is our street" he would yell. These strangers would always turn around and scuttle away as quickly as their legs could carry them. I don't think he was altogether sane. Opposite Algey, lived a little dapper of a man who had a very thick head of grey bristly hair, his hair line protruded almost to his brown bushy eyebrows, he could be seen wearing an old grey suit that had to be at least four sizes too big for him, and he carried a large round biscuit tin under his right arm. He kept chickens at the rear of his dilapidated old house and he limped around the area knocking on doors selling eggs from within his biscuit tin. Sadly, he had a badly deformed left foot from birth, which caused him to walk with a severe limp.

The largest building of all 'down Trosnant' was 'Painters Lodging House'. A four storey property that was used by the American armed forces. Before the war, it was disused and became a play area for the local children. Next to this building lived Dina Pinner who had one son named Donald Henegan. He later became amateur Welter weight boxing champion of Wales.

Opposite lived Victor 'Kipper Foot' Jones and his brother Horace, along with Ken 'Mugsey' Williams. All the families seemed to be related to one another, they were all cousins, The Robinsons', The Williams', The Pinners' and The Jones', very strange!

Our stay with Aunty Marge in April 1945 was a happy one. Their son Michael and I, along with two local lads named Tony Guest and Robert Shannon, spent our days together playing in the 'entry', a covered area to the right of the house. I remember how we teased Tony, pulling his leg and saying "you are only one year old, you've only had one birthday!" as he was born on 29th of February 1940. What bad luck, we thought, a birthday every four years, He took it all in good fun.

It was fairly cramped in the house, but we all got along very well. Dad returned to the mines working with Uncle George. Uncle George was a strong, muscular man with an enormous black hairy chest, which was always on display as he hardly ever wore anything above his waist. He was a soft and friendly man, who would pick Michael and me up at the same time, one on each shoulder. He made us feel so welcome and at home, saying "don't worry about staying with us; you'll have a home of your own one day". Aunty Marge was older than Mam, and she seemed to guide and help her. She had a round pink face that beamed with warmth and love, and she always called me "my Brian". I felt safe and loved. The house was quite strange with a trap door in the centre of the large pantry. It had stone steps leading down to a small cellar where the coal was stored. When the coal scuttle was low, up came the trap door, down went Uncle George, then a large bucket of coal would appear covered in coal dust. He would repeat this several times over until the Coal Scuttle that stood in the hearth was full.

"I think the war will be over soon Taff" Dad said to Uncle George. "I believe so too, Aubrey," he replied. "The Americans and the British are closing in on the Germans at Berlin and the Russians are coming in from the other side through Poland." "But that's only Europe," Dad said. "The war is still raging in the Pacific against the Japanese, but at least the Allies are winning slowly. It will be wonderful to have peace in the world after five long years of war. Although we are not fighting, we're doing what our country needs by mining for coal to keep the industry and the armaments factories going." I listened to this conversation intently and it began to sink in that soon enough it seemed this horrid war was reaching its end. I could not remember what it was like to live in peace time, and I felt a sense of relief and hope, even at my young age. Dad still looked aged and worried, it was obvious that he was concerned with the fact that we still had no home of our own and Mam was almost due to have the baby. Jean, Michael and I would sit and talk about whether the child would be a brother or sister for me, but I still wanted a puppy dog.

Trosnant Pontypool 1947

A few days later, Michael and I were sitting having our breakfast on 'the bench', which was really a long wide length of wood bolted onto the side of a large square wooden table in the centre of Auntie's kitchen. Mam and Dad came down into the kitchen in a hurry and Dad said "Brian, I'm going to take Mam into hospital to have the new baby. Be a good boy for Aunty Marge, Mam will be away for many days."

"I will alright, Mam, Aunty Marge will look after me, I know." She lifted me up into her arms to kiss me goodbye.

A little green van was parked outside with Uncle Reece in the driving seat. Uncle Reece was Dad's youngest brother and he was waiting to take them to the hospital at Llanfrechfa Grange. He had borrowed the van from Norman Jenkins, the owner of a petrol station at Clarence Street, where Uncle Reece worked as a mechanic. The petrol station was on the Clarence and the garage workshop was in a disused foundry at the bottom of Mill Road behind the Clarence Hotel.

In his cheeky voice he yelled "Morning all and how are you Bottle?" as he scooped me into his arms. He always called me that and it always brought a smile to my face. He opened the front door for Mam and let Dad into the back. He gave me and Michael a hug, Jean was in school. "See you all soon," he said as he drove off down Trosnant Street. I stood there, holding Auntie's and Michael's hands until the van went out of sight.

I did not see Dad for a day or two. Aunty Marge and Aunty Esme, Mam's youngest sister, went to visit Mam in hospital and when they came home, they told me I had a little sister called Mary Christine and she was born on the 14th of April. We were so curious and asked what she was like, but Aunty Marge looked very sad. I knew something was wrong and she said that they weren't able to see her as she was very poorly. Thankfully Mam was alright. When Dad came home, I felt very excited as I though everything would be fine. He took me into town where we bought Mam a large bunch of flowers and a card sending our good wishes. Dad went back to work and visited Mam every evening. "When are they coming home to us Dad?" I would ask every night when he came home. Sometimes Uncle George would go along, but even he wasn't allowed to see my new little sister.

A few days later, Dad came home, looking distraught. He placed his arms around me, picked me up and with Aunty Marge, we went into the front room. Dad closed the door behind us and we sat down. "I'm sorry to tell you, Brian, but I want you to be very brave." With tears welling in her eyes, Aunty held my hands while Dad choked out the sorry words he was dreading having to say. "Your little sister Mary has gone to live in heaven with Jesus." "But why can't she live with us?" I said. "Because she was very ill and has gone to sleep forever, Brian."
Dad carried me out of the room and into the kitchen where Jean, Michael and Uncle George were sitting in silence. It seemed as if a huge dark cloud had covered the room everyone was so sad.

Mary Christine died on the 27th of April 1945 and had lived for just thirteen days. She was born with a very bad heart condition and a cleft pallet. She died of heart failure. Poor Mam had never even seen her; Dad was the only one in the family who did. He only ever said that she was beautiful with fair hair. The next day Uncle Reece collected Dad and me and we went to hospital to bring Mam home.

Pontypool Road Station, New Inn in the 1950s

We pulled up outside the hospital main entrance and went inside where we sat on some wooden chairs. Dad went down a corridor to a room and he returned with my mother who looked so tired and weak. She knelt down in front of me and gave me a hug. "I've come to take you home, Mam." "I know you have, Brian. It's good of Uncle Reece to do this for us," she said as he put her small case into the back of the van. "Come on, Bottle. Jump in the back with your Dad and Mam can ride in the front with me." Uncle Reece kept chatting to Mam through the journey home. He tried to raise her spirits by saying that Aunty Marge had cooked a special meal for us all and at least it broke the silence. Our hearts were heavy, we should be filled with excitement bringing a new child home, but instead there was none. No excitement, no expectations and no little Mary Christine for me to play with. I had missed Mam so much and amongst the pain and unhappiness, at least there was a sense of relief that she had come home to us at last.

Mam returned from the hospital still very tired and frail. So she and I stayed for a week or so at Granddad Jones' house at Hanbury Road. Sisters Gwyneth, Dolly, Kathleen and Esme were still living at home and they took care of Mam, making a fuss, which made her feel stronger. We then went back to Aunty Marge's via Peake's bus, the local bus company. By now the funeral arrangements had been made by Dad for the burial of baby Mary at Trevethin churchyard.

On the day of the funeral, a black car pulled up outside Aunty Marge's house. Eddie Rowland's, Aunty Emily's husband, was on leave from the army and carried the tiny white coffin from the car and into the house. It was placed on a small table in the corner of the room where close relatives and the vicar of Mount Pleasant Church stood by. The coffin was blessed and carried into the church which stood around the corner on the road leading to Pontypool. With heavy hearts filled with sorrow, the family gathered, heads lowered and voices silenced.

I stayed behind with Jean and Michael at a lady's house opposite Aunty Marge's. She was called Mrs Salt, but everyone called her Aunty Lucy. We gazed out of her front window until the little coffin and everyone dressed in black had disappeared out of sight and we sat quietly with Aunty Lucy until the women returned from the church service.

Mam and Aunty Marge opened the front door, their faces were sad and sorrow filled their eyes.

"Where's my Dad and our baby gone Mam?" I asked inquisitively. Mam began to cry and Aunty Marge intervened saying "Dad and your uncles have gone to Trevethin churchyard to take Mary to be next to your grandmother Jenkins and now both of them will be in the arms of Jesus."

For the first time, I started crying. And said "Il never see her then, Aunty?" She and Jean then put their arms around me. "We're so sorry, don't cry Brian, you will always have us," they said.

Chapter 3

War Ends In Europe

A few days after the sadness of April, there seemed a sense of happiness in the air. Everyone who owned a radio set had their homes full of people gathering and listening intently to the news coming through. The Russians had entered Berlin and the Americans and British were advancing from the west. Hitler had committed suicide on April 30th and Germany surrendered a few days later we all went on Peake's bus to Granddad Jones' house where all the family had gathered.

Everyone was out in the street singing, cheering, hugging and kissing each other. What a wonderful scene I was witnessing, the air heavy with excitement and relief. War was over and a sense of a new beginning filled our hearts. I enjoyed the electric atmosphere with cousins Colin, Audrey and Pearl.

"What have we won Brian? What is war?" Audrey asked.

"I don't really know what it is, but it must be bad as everyone is happy, drinking and eating sponge cakes now it's over" I replied, a little confused myself.

Granddad Jones said "all we want now is for the boys to come home safe". Mam's four brothers Alf, Albert and Billy were still serving abroad. Jack had returned home and married Aunty Joan in Birmingham. He also reminded everyone of the sadness of Aunty Dolly who was informed by the parents of her boyfriend, Sid Meredith, that he had been killed in action.

Poor Aunty Dolly looked sad among the others, knowing that her boyfriend would never return home.

Later that evening, Mam, Dad and I went over to Aunty Emily's house which was a short walk away at Charlesville. Delight was etched on everyone's faces with cheering and singing taking place. We stayed the night with Aunty and Cousins Margaret and John. I loved to stay there; us three kids would sleep in the same bed and stay up late talking.

"I'm going to be king when I grow up and give everyone plenty of money" John would say.

"No, it's the Prime Minister who gives money away. The king only sits on a gold chair with his family around him in a palace" I would reply, as we pulled the blankets over our heads.

"I want to drive a steam engine and take all the family to the seaside and I also want to go to heaven to see my sister as I didn't see her before she went". I would say.

Our Margaret always wanted to be a film star. " When I grow up, I'm going to sing like Judy Garland in the cinema and everyone will come to see me." She would say.

The one thing the three of us wanted to do together was to hold hands and walk on the moon, where we thought someone lived in a big house. We cuddled up and fell asleep together with all our dreams and wishes…..

Mill Road, viewed from Clarence Street Station

Morning came and with it a sense of hope. Anticipation of a new era filled the minds of the adults in the family. We returned to Aunty Marge's and Dad went to work the afternoon shift with Uncle George, where he overheard someone in the colliery say that their elderly aunt had passed away, leaving her house empty. The house was owned by the Gas Board and Dad decided to make some enquires. Desperate for a home of our own, Dad hoped this would be the one for us as he did not want to return to Halifax.

Later that morning, he went to the Gas Board offices on Clarence Street and returned with a smile on his face.

"They have a cottage which is empty down Mill Road," he said. "The lady who rented it, Mrs Brown, died, but they need to check that the workers don't want it first." Dad seemed to think that as his parents had rented an old house off Mill Road in the past, this would also go in our favour.

"We'll have to keep our fingers crossed, Aubrey," said Mam, "and don't build your hopes up. It's only an old place anyway, but it will be alright."

Two days later, during the morning, Dad said to uncle   "come on, Taff let's go up to the Gas Board and find out about that cottage before we catch the afternoon shift bus."

"I don't think they'll know anything yet," he replied, "I wouldn't be surprised if it's not gone to one of the workers, there are plenty of them. But I'll come with you anyway and we can have a quick pint in the Hanbury pub on the way."

I'm sure Uncle George had high hopes that things were going to work out for us, but at the same time he played things down in case Dad was in for a big disappointment.

Mam sat quietly for the rest of the day. Jean was now in school and Aunty Marge took Michael and me out to Pontypool Park, where we had lots of fun. Later in the evening, Dad and Uncle George returned home from Tirpentwys Colliery, both looking very happy. "We've got the cottage! It's ours; we collect the key tomorrow morning! Sorry we didn't have time to tell you this afternoon."

"Don't worry," said Mam, "that's great news for us all!"

Aunty Marge hugged Mam; she was so pleased for us and was so glad it wasn't very far away. "By the way, Aubrey, what number is it?" Aunty asked.

"Its number 14," Uncle George replied, "14 Mill Road, Mrs Brown's old house, almost at the bottom, next up from Alf Ford who worked in the lamp room."

In the excitement, I don't think Dad cared which house it was. At last it was to be 'our' house.

"How much is the rent?" asked Mam. Dad had been so thrilled that he had forgotten to ask! "They'll tell me when I collect the key tomorrow," he replied as he swept me up into his arms and carried me upstairs to bed, following Uncle George carrying Michael.

"Good night Mam, good night Aunty Marge," I shouted from upstairs. "We're going to see our new house tomorrow, aren't we?"

"Of course we are, Brian. Good night," they replied.

Outside Aunty Marge's house at the top end of Trosnant, the road forked. The road on the right went towards town and the left headed towards Clarence Street, but directly opposite her house was an opening to "Mill

Road". This suddenly dropped steeply and on the left stood a row of seventeen small cottages, all joined together, built the same with two rooms upstairs and two rooms down. The front doors opened out onto a step then directly onto the road as there were no pavements. A large dirty and dusty Gas Works building, with a huge chimney stack which towered above the works was situated behind the cottages. At the bottom of the road was a large area where vehicles turned to return to the top of the hill.

There were a few derelict houses at the bottom one of these, 'The Malt House', being my father's family home before they moved up to Penygarn in 1937. Nearby, there stood a blacksmith's shop which was used as a repair shop for motor vehicles. Later, Uncle Reece would work here as a mechanic. It was owned by Norman Jenkins, who lived in a house near Clarence Street corner called Weighbridge House. This was attached to a petrol station at the entrance to Clarence Street.

Opposite the bottom five cottages at Mill road a refuse tip had begun where the remains of derelict houses stood. Above the tip, a narrow service road ran to the rear of the Clarence Hotel. It passed a milk dairy, the Free Press Printing building and a small bake house called the Carlton Bakery, owned by a man called Mr Barrel.

The next morning was cold but bright. We sat at the kitchen table enjoying our breakfast as Aunty Marge toasted bread in front of the large welcoming fire.

"Come on eat up everyone. Brian, Dad's gone up to the gas board or water board as some people call it. I think it's the same company isn't it, George?" she said.

"I think so love. He's gone up to the offices to fill in some forms and hopefully collect the keys."

"If he does, I expect we will have a busy week in front of us," Aunty Marge replied with an excited tone in her voice. She continued to spread the strawberry jam over the rounds of bread and placed them onto a large plate in the middle of the table. "Come on eat up, Pour the tea out George."

"What will I have to do, Aunty?" I asked puzzled.

"I expect the house will want a damn good clean first, then maybe some painting or whitewashing. There's no electric in those houses, but there is gas so you will probably need some gas mantles."

"What's a gas mantle, Aunty?"

"It's a round flimsy ball thing, open at one end that hooks over a gas flame, fixed in a wall. You turn the gas on and then place a lit match against it. The gas burns inside the mantle which glows bright and lights up the room. They sell them in Bagot's shop."

Bagot's shop was next door up from Auntie's. Old Mrs Bagot would waddle out from behind a large dark blanket that was hung over a length of string separating her living room from the tiny shop. I can only remember her selling a window full of boxes of sweets and Bells Cough Mixture, along with Saxa salt, washing powder and soap. I had never seen any mantles and thought to myself that she must have kept these behind the curtains.

1946 in Pontypool Park, Aunties and Uncles, I'm in front with Cousins, Gean, Michael and Elaine

As I continued to eat my toast and drink my tea, Dad appeared. He didn't have his normal look of sadness about him, but a slight beam of joy and excitement.

"I've got it!" he said, clutching a pair of small brass keys. He walked towards Mam and put his arms around her. "The rent is six shillings a week, plus the water rates, but I don't think that's much. There's a gas meter in there which takes pennies and shillings and we pay the rent weekly at the offices on the Clarence."

"Sounds alright to me, Butty" Uncle George said.

"I'm so pleased for you, Urs," Aunty said, as she hugged Mam.

"Thanks, Marge, for all you've done for us," Mam replied thankfully.

Mam and Dad went upstairs to get ready, and then dressed me so that the three of us could go down to look at the house. The others said they would come down later. With a spring in our step, we left Auntie's and walked across towards Mill Road. The first house belonged to the Davies family, then on past to Tony Guest's House. Tony came out when he saw us walk by, holding an enamel bowl and eating something with a spoon. "Hiya Tone, what's that you're eating?" I asked. "My breakfast," he answered. "Its milk tipped on top of a round of bread, we call it sop. I like it better with warm milk though, but our gas is off because Mam hasn't got any change. Where are you going anyway?"

"We're going down Mill Road as we've got a house there," I said.

"So you'll be leaving Mike's then?"

"Yes, but I'll still be able to play with you, it's only down the hill. Come down and see me when I move."

"Alright Bri, I'll go and tell our Mam I seen you."

I didn't know who lived in the other houses at the time, but before long, I grew to know them all.

We carried on walking past a few more houses until we came to number eight, when a voice called out "Hiya, Aub." It was Roy Lewis, who worked with Dad and Uncle Reece for a time in Coventry at the beginning of the war. He was a short thick set man with black hair combed back flat over his head with Brylcream. He never married and lived alone and he sometimes called Dad Joe, as did some of Dad's other friends. I never knew why, just a nickname, I suppose. "Haven't seen you for a while, mun. Sorry to hear about the baby. See you Saturday, eh?"

"Maybe Roy, I may be busy. We've got a house down here at number fourteen."

"That's Mrs Brown's then. Good old stick she was, salt of the earth. I'm pleased about that for you both." He leaned towards Mam and pecked her on the cheek saying "I'm sure your luck will be better now, Urs." He ruffled my hair and put his hand in his pocket. "Here you are boyo; put this in your money box." He pressed a sixpence into my hand and with his other hand; he pulled out a ration book, ripped out a page and told me to give it to Mam. It was his sweet rations that he wanted Mam to give me. "Thanks mister" I said, looking delighted as I clutched hold of the coin. "I'm rich now!"

"Thanks Roy, come down after we move in. You're always welcome," spoke Dad. "I'll fetch a few flagons of beer with me," Roy replied.

We then passed the Fisher's house at number nine and the Erington's at number ten. Outside their house, a small lorry was parked loaded with compartments of coal. As we passed, it was tipping coal outside the front door and Dad picked me up as we came to huge cloud of dust. The coalman opened his door and leapt out. He was a small man with light blue eyes peering out from his coal covered face. He wore a large welsh 'Dai' cap on his head which looked three sizes too big and was covered in thick black coal dust.

"Bloody sorry about that, Guv, won't be doing this much longer" he said as he emptied the coal onto the road. "It's a bloody mess. Next week we will be delivering 'undred weight sacks. More work for me carrying it into the houses, but it wont leave such a mess on the road. Didn't get any on you did I?"

"No it's alright. I'm moving in to number fourteen soon and don't know if there's any coal in there."

"There is, I delivered a load just before Mrs Brown died." He pointed to a name painted on the door of his lorry. "That's my name, Knights Coal; we're even on the phone now! Give us a ring next time. Got more drops down here fust, number sixteen, Relf's house." Mr Erington opened his front door. He was an elderly grey haired pleasant man and he stood there with a bucket in his hand, ready to begin carrying in the coal.

"Thank you, Mr Knight," he said as he handed him a brown envelope. "Here's your money, don't worry about a receipt." His coal covered hand slid out of his worn leather jacket. He zipped open his money bag which was slung loosely over his shoulder and dropped the envelope safely inside. "Thanks sir, I know it's all there, Mr Erington," he said as he touched the side of his cap as a mark of respect. "See you next time." He went to the front of his lorry and removed a large heavy stone that was placed in front of one of the wheels. "Old handbrake not very good on this steep hill!" he said to dad as he drove down the hill. Dad then spoke to Mr Erington. "I'm moving back here and I've got the keys to number fourteen."

"That's nice Aub, haven't seen you since you left from down the bottom with your Mam and dad to go up to Penygarn. I missed your dad with his old fruit cart. How long since your Mam, Jane died?"

"About two years, Mrs Erington."

"Dad alright?"

"Yes, he still sells fruit and veg from a shop at the back of the house, well it's a large shed really but it's alright and earns him a living. This is my wife Ursula and my son Brian."

"Nice little family Aubrey. Good luck all and see you later, must get on with moving this damn coal."

We walked on down and came by number eleven which was occupied by the Phillips family. There were four children, the youngest being David who was around two years older than me. Their house had flagstones across the front with a small wall at the end that dropped down to the next house. This was ideal for Mrs Phillips as she could sit out on the wall and observe everything that was going on, be it down the road or up. She always knew everything that happened in the lives of her neighbours. She was a plump, round faced lady with tight grey curly hair that seemed shaped like a Banana across her head. She made it her business to never miss a single thing. She knew all the goings on, good and bad. There was nothing to no-one who passed her house without her knowing. If anyone appeared outside talking on a door step, out she would trot, always wearing her black and white spotted apron and carrying a tea cloth in her hand. "How's everybody?" she would ask in her strong Welsh accent, hoping that they would tell her what they were talking about. Everyone called her 'the PBC', which stood for the Phillips Broadcasting Company. But she was a very kind person that everyone loved, always ready to help if she could, and if anyone became ill, she was the first one they would send for. As we passed her house, the curtain moved, then the front door opened, out she came with the tea cloth over her shoulder and she sat on the wall. "Morning! Don't I know you?" she said, pushing her tongue out between her lips. "Of course you do, Mrs Phillips, I'm Aubrey Jenkins."

"Well, it must be ten years since you left here."

"No, it's eight actually," said Dad.

"Who's the boy?"

"It's our son, his name is Brian Anthony this is my wife Ursula," replied Dad as he picked me up proudly in his arms. I was getting a little restless listening to all the chatter. I came level with Mrs Phillips as she sat on the edge of the wall. She thrust her face against mine, squeezed her chubby lips together, and then opened her toothless mouth. "He looks like your Reece. By the way, how are your brothers and sisters?"

"We've been living away during the war. Ted's in the army, Reece works for Norman Jenkins and our Emily's married. Margaret, Joyce and Iris still live at home with Dad and as you probably know, Mam died."

"Yes, I was sorry to hear that, as I liked your Mother Jane, she was a lovely lady. What's brought you down here, Aub?"

"We're coming here to live. I've got the keys to number fourteen, Mrs Brown's old house."

"Well, fancy that, our Albert wanted that place but he's not working and couldn't find the rent. Never mind, you'll be alright with us, Aub. Still no electric here though. You know where I am, Ursula, if you need anything and I mean that. Well, anything apart from money, that is." She said this sincerely and with a somewhat sad little chuckle. "Just tap on the door."

"Thank you, Mrs Phillips, that's very kind of you," Mam moved towards her and clasped her hand. "It's nice to have someone like you nearby. I expect there'll be something we'll need pretty soon."

We then passed number twelve where Mr and Mrs Young and their daughter Beryl lived and then onto the Smith's at number thirteen.

Chapter 4

Fourteen Mill Road

As we came to number 14, we stood back and surveyed the front of the cottage. There was a small window on each side of the front door and two above the bedrooms. In front of the door was a large worn step that curved in the centre due to years of wear and scrubbing. I'm not sure why, but most women in Mill Road and Trosnant felt it necessary to scrub their front door step every day. They thought people would gossip about them if they didn't. Dad shook the front windows and said "not too bad, but I think they could do with a lick of paint. Front door's alright, nice colour green. I believe this is a new door recently fitted, well, about a year or two ago." He smiled as he took the keys from his pocket, unlocked the door and pushed it open. The dark room flooded with light as Mam opened the curtains that had been left hanging there. From the ceiling, thin shafts of light shone through the gaps in the open beam floorboards that seemed to point down at the uneven flagstones covering the floor.

The room was empty and bare with a cold damp smell about it. To the right stood a large black cast iron fire place with an oven door. Ashes still filled the fire grate with a long black fender holding back any that attempted to escape and cover the floor. The whole fireplace was huge, almost filling the entire wall. To the left of the fireplace, a small door hung open. I could see some steps twisting around leading upstairs. I opened a door on the left of the front room which led into another room that faced the road. It was very small and had a little fire grate in the corner. The tiny room looked so dark and dismal and the brown wallpaper added to the feeling of darkness. At once, Mam opened the heavy curtains to let in some desperately needed light, but it still looked just as bad. A door to the left led into a large pantry, on the back wall was the back door which opened out down some steps onto a small yard.

A door to the right of the yard brought us to the toilet and a door on the left led to the lean-to area that we called the scullery or coal house. Coal was stored on the right and on the left was a cold water tap that came out of the wall and underneath stood a large enamel bucket. A large flat piece of wood positioned on top of a gas boiler that served as a worktop then an old gas cooker stood next to the bucket. "There's plenty of coal here," Dad said positively, as he kicked back some cobbles that had tumbled onto the kitchen floor. Mam turned on the gas taps and bent down to listen for any gas that may have been escaping. "They left this cooker here, it's a bit old but very clean, suppose it will do," she said as she opened the oven door and looked inside. "I don't think this gas is turned on, there should be a gas tap by the front door, I'll turn it on in a minute," Dad said, "I wonder if the water is on?" Dad turned on the tap and out gushed water into the bucket below. "Water's on, Urs!" he said with a giggle.

"I want a wee, Mam!" I said, clutching my trousers.

"That's the lav by there in that door. Wait a second until I see if it's alright." She walked towards the lavatory door and opened it, looked inside and pulled the chain as the water flushed down.

"There's no gas light in here, so we'll have to carry a torch with us when we come out here, and when we go to the scullery. There is a gas light in there so we'll keep a box of matches by the cooker."

As we stood in the yard, my father picked me up to look over the wall that separated us from the gas works. "Must we look at those dirty sheds and chimney stacks?" I spoke the words of an infant who thought someone could sweep a magic wand over the night scene and replace it with sparkling coloured rainbows. Mam answered "It's not much better looking from the front door, as the tip is facing right at us." She glanced inside the coal house and spoke negatively, "I suppose I'm expected to cook in there, am I?" A sad look of despair swept over Dad's face. He didn't think she would complain, but only be too glad to be on our own in a place that would be made our home. "I can brighten it up" he said as he put me down onto the yard. "I can whitewash the yard and in here in the cooking area."

Mam didn't answer him and we went inside. My mother always showed her distaste when she was unhappy. Dad's feelings had obviously been deeply hurt. He looked at the stairs door. "Let's go upstairs" he said, with a feeling of anxiety in his voice, hoping my mother would be pleased about something.

My mother went up first, then me and then Dad. The tiny twisting steps came straight into the first bedroom. There was no door or landing. The room had a small window facing out to the front. I walked slowly into the next bedroom, which was to be mine, and felt as if I was being a brave boy to be the first to look around. The floor was covered in dark red oil cloth and the walls were adorned with green paint. There was a gas lamp on the wall, looking pathetically bare without a shade to cover it.

I sat on the low window sill and peered out from the window. I could see the tip clearly. It was mostly covered with coke and ash and above this; I could see a milk bottling plant called Cambrian Dairy, the Free Press printing rooms and the Carlton Bakery. The rear of the Clarence Hotel stood proudly next to these buildings towards the right.

"I like this bedroom, Mam," I called out. "Is it mine?"

"Yes, I expect so. This room in here is dangerous anyway. You could easily fall down those stone stairs and hurt yourself," she said as she came in and sat beside me on the window sill. Dad came in and sat on the floor and chatted about what they had to get before we could move in. "Floor covering in here is alright, don't you think? It was nice of them to leave it, but I think we will have to get some for the bedroom in there. Oil cloth like this would be fine, I think, and an off-cut would probably do."

"Yes, that would be ok. All we need up here is a small bed for Bri, a double for us, a wardrobe, a chest of drawers and some curtains."

We then went back downstairs. My mother looked around the room and Dad peered into the dark pantry. "Pretty big in here, plenty of shelves to keep everything on. Pity there's no light though. I expect the light from the room will be ok when the pantry is open."

"I've found some matches, turn on the gas," my mother said, as she picked up a box of matches from a shelf that was fixed underneath the gas light. "This is a handy place to keep them, especially when we come into the house when it's dark." Dad went to the corner of the room, bent down in front of the window and turned the large gas tap that was positioned close the ground. "Try it, Urs." Mam turned the tap underneath the gas light, stuck a match and placed it near the flimsy mantle. There was a slight bang as the gas lit from a small hole in the mantle. Dad decided to clear the fireplace of all the ashes and he retrieved an old bucket and brush from the outside yard, then he decided to light the fire to help dry out the house. "There's some firewood stacked in the pantry on the floor and there's some old newspapers in there as well," said Dad. "There's also a broom. I'll have a sweep around," said Mam.

Later that day, Aunty Marge came to the house with Jean and Michael to have a look around. We returned to Auntie's later in the evening, where Mam and Dad talked about purchasing some furniture to help make the house a home for us. Dad said he was going to see Mrs Jevans to see what she had stored, while Mam and Aunty would go into town to look in the shops. Even though the war had ended, times remained hard with very little money or furniture around, apart from 'utility furniture', which was made quickly and cheaply. This suited Mam as we had very little money to spend.

Placed at the bottom of Mill Road was a pathway that led up to the Newport to Pontypool road. The path also led to a large second hand furniture warehouse, known as 'Jevans' Stores'. It was a large old building that used to be corn merchants. Every time someone entered the store, a bell would ring loudly above their head, alerting Mrs Jevans to her incoming customers. The first glance inside was of complete darkness, until the large door opened wide to reveal a room with no windows, but filled with furniture and household goods stacked up high.

The Clarence Hotel, Pontypool

"Old Mrs Jevans" who owned the store, sat at the rear of the room in a brown leather studded chair that swivelled around. She bought used household goods which she stored until someone came along and wished to purchase them at a profit. She was a short plump lady who wore a black felt hat upon her head that fell tight down over her ears, reminding me of an American GI's helmet. She also wore a large, heavy grey coat with a grey fur collar and black boots. Her money was kept about her person in a brown cloth holdall positioned over her shoulder protectively.

In the corner of the huge room stood a dusty wooden table and upon it was a kettle positioned upon a gas ring. She would often boil water from this to make her tea throughout her working day. Also on the table stood a large wooden lockable box with a few books inside. This is where she kept her accounts and she would make her entries meticulously each time an item was bought or sold. I cannot recall where she actually lived or if she had any family at all. All I did know is that she appeared at 10 o'clock each day opened the door and closed at precisely at 5 o'clock and then promptly disappeared. Each time someone came to her store to sell her some goods, she would waddle out, take a good look at the item observing all she could, give a price and that was that, in a take it or leave it kind of manner. No one would dare bargain with her and in most cases they would promptly accept without any attempt to persuade a better deal. She would then ask them to bring it into the store. Never would she carry anything herself. If someone wanted to purchase an item, they would look around and ask her for a price. She would offer this firmly with her air of authority but sometimes she did actually accept an offer. Then they would have to clear the way and carry the item out of the store themselves without any help from Mrs Jevans.

Dad went along to Jevans store and bought a metal framed double bed, a wardrobe and a chest of drawers. On his return, he pleasingly announced "They are like new" and he and Uncle George carried them into our new home. Mam and Dad also went into town and bought some linoleum for the first bedroom which Dad and Uncle George cut and fitted. My mother bought a new mattress for the bed from Bevan's furniture shop in Pontypool. I already had a small bed of my own from Auntie's.

"Well, that's upstairs done, Urs. What next do you think?" Dad asked.

"Your sister Emily has two armchairs, she replied we could have, and Reece said he would be happy to collect them for us in his van 'she replied.

"I know they are very nice, brown leatherette with wooden arms. She must be buying a new suite then?"

"Yes she told me she was. I think by giving us those chairs, it's an excuse to buy herself all new!"

"It's only a table and some chairs we need for now. Mrs Jevans has a decent set for five shillings, what do you think of that?" Dad enquired.

Mum replied "I'll go and take a look at them tomorrow and if they're alright, then they'll do for now until we can afford new. Marge and I are going into town to buy some cutlery and frying pans, a kettle and a tea pot."

We had such little back then, but we were grateful to anyone who offered help and cherished the things we were lucky enough to afford to have. My mother did buy the table and chairs the next morning and Dad and Uncle George collected them later that day. Mam came home with the required kitchen utensils which she stored in the pantry and Uncle Reece brought the two chairs from Aunt Emily's in his van. He also brought a large oval tin bath from an ironmonger called Brimfield's, which was based in an area known as Wainfelin on the outskirts of town. Mr Brimfield had a van from which he travelled around the local areas selling his goods. The bath was around five feet long and three feet wide and Dad hung it on the wall in the yard next to the kitchen door. Number fourteen was almost ready for us to move into.

"I believe we can move next Saturday morning Marge, if that's alright with you," my mother said as she and Aunty sat by the fire chatting about the things that we needed. "Of course you can, I can't see any problems with that, We can carry all your clothes down in the morning and if you need any washing done in a day or two, you can bring it up to me, we can go into town shopping for some food to begin stocking your pantry and if there's any more that you need, you can pop up to my house"

"Thanks, Marge. I don't know what I would have done without you," my mother said, as she put her arms around her and gave her hug. "We haven't got a lot of money left, just enough for a week's food"

"So that's it!" Dad said, "Saturday we move out, ok George?"

"That alright mun, sounds good to me boyo" he answered.

Saturday the 16th of June 1945, Mam and Dad started packing our belongings and putting them carefully into cardboard boxes. I sat and had some breakfast with Michael and Jean and when the packing had been done, we all began walking together with boxes in our hands, down to our new home at Mill Road.

Our walk was filled with excitement and anticipation as a new chapter in our lives was about to begin. As we entered, we placed our boxes upon the table and Dad started cleaning the grate and laying the fire, while my mother and Aunty started putting the clothes into the wardrobe and the chest of drawers upstairs and made the beds. Our beds in our new home, how comforting that sounded. Jean had carried some milk, tea and sugar in a small carrier bag and Uncle George offered to boil the kettle on the gas cooker in the outhouse, and make us all some tea. We all sat around the table, enjoying our first cup of tea in our new house. Mam and Aunty went to Pontypool market to do some shopping and Dad and Uncle George went back up to Auntie's to collect the rest of our things.

As the evening grew cold, my father lit the fire and we sat in front of it, Dad sitting in one chair holding me close and Mam in the other chair. Feelings of contentment filled me and I truly felt happy and secure in the hub of a safe family environment, with Mam and Dad. I put my bed clothes on and Dad carried me on his back up the narrow twisting stone staircase, through his bedroom and into my own. It felt cold and quite damp, and it was bare with just my small bed in the corner. I sat on the window ledge for a moment looking out at the bleak view of the tip. I could hear the sound of some children playing at the bottom of the road and became inquisitive, looking forward to going down in the morning to see who they were.

Dad tucked me into bed and kissed me "Goodnight Bri, see you in the morning" he said, and as he left and closed the door behind him, I now felt very lonely. I said my prayers as I did every night. "God bless my granddads, Mam and Dad, Aunties and Uncles, cousins Michael Jean John and Margaret". Still feeling alone in this unfamiliar room, I searched for some toys in the toy box under my bed. Out came a small grey teddy bear that I had named Ted and a little black Scottie dog which was around six inches long that I called Blackie. I held them close to me under my blankets and I always imagined them talking to me and telling me that one day, all my family would live in a big house together, on a hill overlooking the town. Dad and Uncle George would have plenty of money and wouldn't need to go down the mines anymore and I would answer my toys saying that they could come with me and stay in my big warm bedroom. I fell asleep with my happy thoughts in my mind.

As I awoke the next morning, my bedroom door was still closed. I gazed around the room still damp and cold and I put Ted and Blackie under my arm. I stepped towards the light that flooded through the small window and opened the curtains slightly to look out at the tip. It was a bright Sunday morning and I could see some small boys collecting some things from the tip. It looked like they were placing small grey stones into their buckets and any pieces of wood they found among the rubble, they put in a pile at the bottom. When the buckets were full, they went out of sight to the left down to the house at the bottom of the road. I wondered who they were and what they were doing.

Mill Road in the winter of 1947 — our house can be seen second from the left behind the telegraph pole

The silence of my room was broken by the large latch on the door springing open with a loud clatter. The door opened with Mam's face popping around. "You alright? Didn't know you were awake, sleep alright? What are you looking at?"

"Some boys out on the tip" I replied. My mother looked out of the window, "Oh that's the Trinders from the bottom house" she said. "They have been picking cokes. The council ash lorry sometimes empties their loads there after their collections around Pontypool. The coke is good to re-use on a house fire and they search among the ashes and rubble and put the cokes into their buckets. They also collect any wood they find then go into their house and light the fire if it's cold."

I put Ted and Blackie carefully back into my little toy box and went downstairs. As a child, Sundays were always special to me as Dad did not go to work down the mines. He was busying himself clearing the ashes with a bucket from the fireplace. He then went out into the yard; put the ashes into a round wooden box that had a mesh bottom which allowed the ashes to travel through leaving just the small cokes in the box. "What's that, Dad?" I said inquisitively

"It's a coke riddle; the coke that stays in the box can be used again on the fire."

"Like the ones the Trinders collected off the tip?"

"Yes that's right."

My mother went out to the outhouse which was what we used to call the kitchen, to get some breakfast. "First day in our new house today, Bri. What would you like to eat?"

"Some toast with jam on it please Mam, with warm milk, if we have any."

"The milkman left us a pint on the door step this morning, He must have heard that we had moved in, same milkman as Aunty Marge, I think."

Each time my mother had to boil or cook anything, she had to carry it out of the pantry then outside to the outhouse where the gas cooker stood. If the coal fire was lit in the room, we could boil a kettle and make our toast by using a large pronged fork carefully holding the bread against the bars of the fire. Sometimes we also used the black iron oven to the right of the fire if it was still warm in the morning.

After breakfast I asked my mother if I could go out onto the road and play and she agreed but I was to go no further than the Gas lamp post that stood opposite Trinders house, and not up the road or onto the tip. I dare not as I knew she would be watching me. As I gingerly opened the front door, I glanced up and down the road and cast my eyes over the grey unsightly looking tip which loomed in front of me. I began to think to myself, is this really my new place to live? My eyes rested upon the large empty blacksmiths shop that stood firmly to the left of the tip. I began to walk past the house next door where Mr and Mrs Ford and their son Ken lived and it was all so quiet. That was until I came to number sixteen where a boy came out and spoke to me.

"Hi. You gona to live down here?"

"Yes, we came here yesterday."

"What's your name?" he asked, Brian Jenkins I answered.

"Mam" he yelled, "There's a new boy here, and his name is Jenkins."

A lady then came out and said "Hello, is your Dad Aubrey?" yes I answered

"My name is Mrs Relf, I knew your Dad and his family when they lived opposite years ago in the old Malt house, it's a shame but it's all buried now." She pointed to a derelict building slowly disappearing under the tip.

"Yes, Dad told me."

The boy who was about my age informed me that his name was Terry and said he had three sisters Doreen, Valerie and Jean. He said that the girls went to school but not today as it was Sunday. They had gone to the park with his

Dad, but Terry hadn't gone as he wanted to play on his scooter. "Have you got a scooter?" He asked.

"No" I replied.

"You can have a go of mine if you like" and he pulled a shiny green scooter through his front door. "Mam said I must not go past the Gas lamp post so I will have a go another time."

"Alright mun, see you later" and he ran up the hill, turned around and climbed on his scooter. With both feet firmly in place, he came speeding past me and on to the large open area at the bottom of the road.

I slowly walked by the bottom house and noticed it was much lower than all the other houses. It almost seemed sunk in the ground. You had to go down a few steps to the front door and it had a narrow passage running along the front of the property. I could see straight into the bedroom windows as they were level with my eye line. Just then, two boys came out from the side of the house. They were the same boys I had seen earlier picking things from the tip. They were both wearing black rubber Wellingtons causing a red ring below their knees where they had been rubbing against their legs making them look quite sore.

"Hello, I think I saw you this morning from my bedroom window, collecting cokes from the tip." I spoke in a most friendly manner as I didn't know what to expect.

"Yes, it was me and our Dennis," spoke the older one. "We had to lay the fire this morning. My name is Billy, Billy Trinder.

The Trinder family seemed to be the poorest down the road. Orlando, Dolly, and their eight children, five above my age; Betty, Tommy, Billy and Terry. Dennis was around my age Anise Margaret and Michael, were the younger ones. I often wondered how they all slept in just two tiny bedrooms. They were all very friendly to me and I used to go in and out of their home as if it were mine. They all used to wear Wellington boots, even in the summer months as well as in winter, and when they got too small to wear, they were handed down to the next one that they fitted.

"I'm Dennis, what are you doing down here?" said the other lad.

"I live down here now, in that house up there," I answered as I pointed to number fourteen.

"O aye and what school dew go to, got any brothers?"

"I don't go to school yet, not old enough and I haven't got any brothers or sisters."

"We do all go to Pontymoile School. Anise Margaret and our Michael are all too young. Wonu play football?"

"I can't, Mam said I mustn't go past your house."

"Well, we'll have a kick on the road then! Terry, bring the ball out - there's a new kid out year. His names Brian and he lives in Brown's house."

Out came a scruffy boy about my age carrying a small beat up dirty ball that was in need of inflating. "Hello dew play with a ball then, we could do with a new one, our Dad said our Tommy could go and buy one from Woolwus up in town next week. If our Dad had a good week out from the foundry, that is. You got a ball, Bri?"

"Yes Terry, but I haven't seen it since our Mam took me to the park in Halifax."

"Halifax, where's that?" asked Terry.

"Somewhere where we lived in Yorkshire."

He shrugged his shoulders as if to say he didn't have a clue where this was. A voice came from the house. It was Mrs Trinder. "Mind what you do with that little boy, he only looks about five." The boys looked at me strangely. "I'm five, how old are you then?" asked Dennis.

"Nearly five," I answered.

"I am six," Terry said.

"And I am nearly eight," Billy said proudly.

After we kicked the ball about for a while, we sat down on the steps that led down to their house. Tommy and Betty came out to talk to me. Then I heard my mother's voice coming from up the road.

"Brian, are you alright?" She came down and began chatting to Mrs Relf and Mr and Mrs Trinder. They hoped she would be happy living down Mill Road and if they could be of any help to her, all she had to do was ask. Although they were very poor, these people were very caring and were happy to welcome us to this new place.

We went back up to the house and I was feeling so happy, thinking of all the new friends I had to play with. Sunday dinner was cooking and we all sat down to enjoy our first meal together.

Mr and Mrs Ford and their son Kenny were our other neighbours, with Kenny being slightly older than me. Mrs Ford worked down at Weston's Biscuit Factory and she loved to sing. She could often be heard singing over the wall that separated our house from hers. She had a wonderful voice and sang while she carried out her chores. Her hair was very beautiful, shiny and black and she always appeared very smart. We would sit and listen to her sing her songs and always clap our hands after each one had been sung. Mam would make a pot of tea and hand her a cup over the wall. Life was happy and I was content, my mother taking me into town shopping and calling into Aunty Marge's where I would spend time playing with my cousins. The summer was warm and bright and I spent my days enjoying the outdoors. I would take a bath in the big tin bath outside in the yard and wait for Dad to come home from the mines.

The tip opposite was always a constant menace though, with rats appearing scurrying around, for waste food that had been tipped out, some men would appear and shoot at them with small bore rifles.

My fifth birthday was approaching and Dad asked me what I would like. "I don't mind, Dad, I don't know what I want "Alright then, I tell you what, let it be a surprise," he said.

"Ok then, Dad," was my answer.

Monday, August the 6th arrived and I ran downstairs excited to see what my present may be. I ate my breakfast and opened my cards and Mam explained that Dad had left for work but had left me a present in the pantry. I rushed out to the panty and there I found a bright green wooden scooter. Dad had bought it from a local carpenters shop next up from Norman Jenkins' garage. They made everything you could think of at the shop, but mainly they sold windows and coffins. Within seconds I was out on the road showing all my new friends my fantastic new present. Mam had to help me at first, but by the time Dad came home, I could go all the way down the road on my own. The day got better and better as Mam and Dad held a birthday party for me on the small grassy area opposite our house. It was nice summer evening and all the kids and parents of the neighbourhood came, bringing tables and chairs of their own. The children played happily while the grownups engaged in more serious conversation. America had dropped an atomic bomb upon the city of Hiroshima in Japan which had resulted in many thousands of people losing their lives. Three days later, a second bomb was dropped over Nagasaki and this signalled the true end of the Second World War with the surrender of Japan.

Chapter 5

Park Terrace School

One evening soon after my birthday, Mam and Dad sat down with me and said they had something very important to say to me. I curled up in one of the armchairs clad in my pyjamas, not sure what they were about to come out with.

"Brian, it's nearly September and you must start school now." Dad spoke with a kind but firm voice. "I am going to try and get you into Park Terrace School. It's a little out of the area but it is a very good school."

"But I don't want to go there, all the other kids on Mill Road go to Pontymoile School."

"Yes I know, but I don't think it's a very good school. I went there and so did our Reece and Ted and they can't hardly read or write." I sat in silence. "Just try Park Terrace. Michael is going and Jean has already started, and you can still play with the others when you come home."

"Alright Dad, I can call for our Mike on the way." With this news, I opened the latch on the door and went up the tiny stairs to my bed. I cuddled Blackie and Ted under the blankets and told them that I would be going to Park Terrace School. In my mind, they answered me back saying that they wished they could come along with me.

The following few days, my mother and Aunty Marge took Michael and me into Pontypool town shopping for some new school clothes. On the morning of the 3rd of September, my mother dressed me in new grey trousers, grey shirt and pullover and a little woollen tie with wide black and grey stripes running across. Park Terrace School was unique in the area for it was a two storey building with a playground upon the roof. High railings travelled all along the roof to protect the children. An old Victorian school once stood on the site, but this had since been demolished making way for the new school which was built in 1936. A ten minute walk took me from our house in Mill Road, up to the Clarence, on to Lower Bridge Street and over the railway line bridge which led to the school. Little did I know back then that one day I would live at 21 Lower Bridge Street.

Mrs Humphries, the first year teacher didn't seem to like me very much. One day at the beginning of term, she hit me hard across my ear for talking to some of the other children in class. When my mother picked me up later that day she could see that I was fraught and not myself. She asked what the matter was and I showed her my ear which was red and sore. She marched me straight back into school and demanded to see my teacher. Mam gave her such a telling off and threatened that if this happened again she would report her to the Headmaster, Mr Clever. Mam was only a small lady but she could surely frighten the living daylights out of anyone that crossed her. After that incident Mrs Humphries acted differently towards me and I was glad that Mam had stood up to her.

1950 School photo at Park Terrace School

As we got older and more responsible, Michael and I would walk to and from school together on our own. We went to Aunty Marge's home for our lunch where she would cut the bread so thin you could actually see through it. I used to love eating there. We would wait at the top of Trosnant for my mother and Aunty to come home from shopping, have our dinner and then return to school. A few months later, I became puzzled as Michael went into Mr Montgomery's class, which was separated from the rest of the school children. I found out later it was a class for pupils with learning difficulties.

We always visited Granddad Jones' regularly at Cwmffrwdoer. There were still many girls still living at home - Aunts Esme Gwyneth and Dolly and Uncle Derek. However, it was starting to fill up again, with Billy returning home from the Air Force. Alf was now married to Aunty May, Albert came home during the war and married Aunty Ann.

Uncle Jack got married at the end of the war at Yardley Birmingham to Aunty Joan. Uncle Billy told me stories of flying missions over Germany and about Uncle Alf whose ship was sunk by German fire in the Baltic Sea, while shipping supplies to the Russians. By the time he was rescued, he had suffered severe frostbite in his feet and was unable to walk. He had to spend months in a military hospital and was later sent home. He could not continue his job as a bricklayer, but obtained a job on the railways. Uncle Billy returned to the coalmines. Before the war, the five boys worked at the same place one after another as butcher boys at the local cooperative meat shop.

As Christmas approached, we all grew very excited. Granddad Jenkins had received a letter from Uncle Ted who was Dad's older brother, informing him that he would be returning from his duties in the army. He was the only one from the Jenkins family to do military service and he was to be demobbed from Hereford barracks on Friday, the twenty first of December. He had been in the army for the past five years and had never married or had any Lady friends all his life.

All the family were very excited at the prospect of his return. Reece said he would collect him from Pontypool Road Station at about two o'clock and bring him home to Penygarn. Mam, Dad and I went up to the house in Penygarn early that morning with Aunt Emily, Margaret, John and the other three sisters. Margaret, Joyce and Iris had decorated the house with welcome home banners. Granddad Jenkins didn't share our excitement, he felt more anxious and rather sad as he thought about the things that had occurred while his son was away. The loss of his wife Jane two years earlier was especially poignant and he was nervous about the reunion not knowing what to say or expect when he came home. He sat in his armchair looking pale and uneasy, his bald head and thick grey moustache twitching in anguish.

Cousin Margaret had been just two years old when Ted had left for the war and to her and us nephews, John and I, he was a stranger. We all stood smartly in our best clothes, waiting for Reece's van to appear. "Here it is," yelled Aunt Emily with much excitement. Down the road it came and pulled outside the house. "Don't crowd him," said Dad. "Wait in line on the pavement." Reece got out, walked around and opened the passenger door. "Welcome home Ted," he said. A very slight man appeared with thin features, sparse black hair combed tightly back and he looked tired and gaunt. He wore a black pinstriped suit with a white shirt, no tie and his collar looked around three sizes too big for him. Ted was thirty three years old, but to me he looked much older. What effect did this terrible war have on him? Maybe we would find out in time to come. "Welcome home," Dad said, as he tenderly put his arms around him, fighting back the tears that were streaming down his cheeks. "Hi Aub," he said in a frail voice. "It was sad to hear about our Mam passing away, and you and Ursula losing the baby. I read about it in Dad's letters."

"I know, we will visit their graves later on." Dad stood aside, and then the four sisters rushed forward and hugged him affectionately. He looked so frail amongst them.

As the commotion was taking place, John and I stood quietly on the pathway leading to the front of the house, not quite knowing what to do. We were dressed in our cream silk shirts and short black trousers and Margaret was clad in her new pink dress. "Is this our Emily's girl, Margaret?" Ted asked as he bent down to pick her up. "She's grown into a lovely kid." She frowned at him, not remembering who he was. "I'm Uncle Ted." He glanced across at us and said "They must be my nephews, Brian and John." We stood still and silent wondering what to do but just then, he came over, bent down and hugged the two of us. "I got some home made sweets in my haversack that I managed to buy in Hereford market. Give ew um after, kids, when I open my bag."

Uncle Reece carried the bag from the van, through the archway and into the rear of the house, everyone followed. Ted entered first, through the back door which led into the kitchen. He walked slowly towards the large table in the centre of the room which had benches on each side and some "Bakers" chairs all around. Granddad sat in his large wooden armchair in front of a roaring fire. "Hi Dad," Ted said as he walked across the room to put his arms around him. Tears filled both their eyes. "Hello son, it's been a long time. I'm glad you made it home safe and for Christmas as well. You look a lot thinner than when you left!"

"Yes I know Dad, but I'm home safe and that's all that matters. A lot of my mates were not as lucky as me. I lost many good friends." He placed his hands over his face to cover the tears that welled in his eyes. Granddad turned to us all, as if he were grateful to have his family around him. Uncle Ted had obviously been deeply affected by the war, much more so than the rest of us. "Come on you lot, make our Ted a nice cup of tea!" With that, the ladies of the family had a mad rush towards the kettle. They all laughed and let our Iris make the tea as she was the youngest, us kids sat on the settee mesmerised by the strange looking haversack, knowing that there were sweets inside. Soon Ted came in and took off his coat, undid his collar and took off his thick wide belt. He hung them upon the nail behind the door that led to the small hallway which in turn led to the front door and stairs to the bedrooms. He sat down, took off his boots and glanced at the sack and then at us. "Guess you kids want to know where those sweets are?" We nodded with silent anticipation as he picked it up and stood it between his legs. He opened the cord at the top and pulled some clothes out, put them on the floor, then opened a brown paper bag which contained three white paper bags. He gave one to each of us and inside we found a mixture of boiled sweets made by someone at the Hereford market. "Thank you!" we said and then he went upstairs to wash. They were lucky to have a bathroom inside the house. "Nice man," said Margaret. "He must be a nice man, he's our uncle" answered John.

Later that day, Reece took Aunt Emily home with Margaret and John and I sat at the back of his van and enjoyed the journey. I stayed with them for the weekend as school had ended for the Christmas holidays. On the Sunday, Uncle Ted came to visit us at Auntie's and we caught Peake's bus back home to Mill Road. Dad and Ted spoke about his plans for the future.

"What are you going to do now that you have left the army Ted?" Dad asked him,

"I suppose I will have to go back down the mines again."

"Well, there's still plenty of coal down there I can assure you."

"I know, but I would like to do something different. You know I can hardly read or write. Dad is still selling fruit and veg from the shed at the back of the house, but that's just enough to support him."

Mam came in with a tray of tea and a plate of sandwiches, handed them to Ted and said "Maybe you could start selling fruit and veg from your Dad's old cart just like he used to. It's still over in the field."

"That's an idea Urs, but to be honest, me and horses don't get on that well!"

"You used to drive vehicles in the army, you can drive a van, can't you?"

"Yes, but you need money for one, and they are scarce now because of the war, Anyway, I've a few weeks to think about what I'm going to do." With that, he left to catch the 9.30 bus home from the Clarence bus stop. "By the way, our Dad's still not very well. He complained about chest pains this morning, so I had better make a move. Its Christmas Eve tomorrow and

I want to do some shopping in town. I will call down if Dad's any worse, Aubrey, will I see you Christmas day?

"Yes, we hope so. Ursula's shopping tomorrow and I'm staying in to look after Brian."

"Goodnight Urs, goodnight Aub, see you," he spoke cheerfully.

Dad stood on the door and watched Uncle Ted walk slowly up Mill Road. He looked a lonely figure walking though the darkness through the dimly lit night; with the only light coming from a gas lamp that stood on the slight bend half way up Mill Road. The only other light that shone was another gas lamp that stood at the bottom opposite the Trinders' home.

The next day Dad and I put up some Christmas decorations while my mother went shopping. It was so exciting for me to be enjoying such a special time of year in our new home. I told Dad of my worries over Father Christmas not being able to come down our chimney, but Dad reassured me that he was magic and not to worry too much. Mam came home and began cooking. The wonderful aroma of Christmas food filled the kitchen and drifted through the house. "Don't forget the mince pies, Mam," I said. "I can leave one by the fire place for Father Christmas to enjoy. He may be hungry on such a busy night delivering everyone's presents."

My father and I got ready to go into town to buy my mother a special gift from us both. She asked us to be careful as town was busy with the hustle and bustle of people rushing around buying last minute presents and food for Christmas day. She also said there was quite a bit of traffic about too. Dad and I looked around the shops and in the market. Dad bought Mam a large clock that would sit on the mantelpiece above the fireplace. He bought it from Billy Saddler's stall that he used to know before the war. Dad had a fruit and veg stall himself for a little while when he left school.

"It's yours for five bob, give me two now and pay me the rest at a tanner a week. That alright, Aub?" he said when Dad enquired about the price.

"Yes that's great Bill, thanks. Will you wrap it up for me? I don't want the missus seeing it." He was happy to sell it at a good price as he knew Dad well and was aware that he didn't have a lot of money. "You were a good friend to me before the war began. You always gave me your damaged fruit and sold me veg at a cheap price - I don't forget good deeds." He said those words with pure feeling and he was happy to repay a favour to someone who had shown him kindness in the past. He pulled some pretty paper from a roll and said we could have this free. "Nice boy you got there Aub, yours is he?" He said as he ruffled my hair.

"Yes, this is our Brian."

"Where's your Ted now?"

"He came home from the army on Wednesday. He's alright; he's at home helping out with Dad's grocery shop at the back of the house at Penygarn. Dad's not very well, pains in his chest, but our Margaret and Joyce are still at home taking care of him and he says he'll go to the doctor after Christmas." Dad handed over a two shilling piece. "Thanks Bill, I'll pay you the rest as soon as I can."

"I know, have a nice Christmas, Aub you're the best."

Dad was always well liked wherever he went. A true gentleman with a good kind heart. We walked around town and bought Mam a Christmas and birthday card as it was her birthday as well on Christmas day along with a few other small things, then started to walk home. "Don't tell Mam about her present mind, Bri. It's not only a special Christmas surprise but a birthday surprise too."

"How old is she, Dad? I forgot." He bent down and spoke to me quietly. "Twenty nine, but don't tell anyone. Women don't like to talk about their age."

"Aunty Marge is thirty one, our Mike told me."

"Ok then, but don't tell anyone."

"How old are you then Dad?"

"Never you mind! We are nearly home, I'll go straight into the pantry to hide the clock when we get in."

"What if she sees you?"

"If she does, it doesn't matter that much, as the present is wrapped up. She'll have guessed that we went to town to get her a present anyway."

We passed by Aunty Marge's house and Michael came rushing out. "What's that under your arm, Uncle Aubrey?

"Never mind Mike, it's a surprise for Aunty Ursula.

"I'm not allowed to say Mike, but I'll tell you tomorrow on Christmas Day when we come up to your house."

Dad popped his head around Auntie's door and called to see if Uncle George was alright. "Yes, all the shopping's done. Will I see you in the bar of the Clarence hotel later or in the Hanbury?"

"I expect so, if she will let me out, mun!" Dad said jokingly. "Our Reece will sure to be in the bar of the Clarence hotel, so if I do go out, I will be in there with him."

"Alright Aub."

"May see you later Marge, and if not I'll see you tomorrow."

"Can't come out Aub, I'm busy cooking!" she answered.

"I know that, I'm off now anyway. See you."

We walked down Mill Road and Dad was surprised to see Reece's van parked opposite our house. We went inside and Reece was sat talking to my mother. She looked up and said "Hello both, shopping done? I'll put the kettle on and make some tea for us."

"Hi Reece, everything alright?" Dad spoke in a worried tone as he began to frown.

"It's Dad, he's not very well. I thought you should know. He still has pains in his chest and the doctor came and said he thinks he's had a mild heart attack. His heart is pretty weak. He has had some tablets but he made it clear that he would not go into hospital. Not with Ted coming home and it being Christmas."

Mam came in with a tray of teas. "It's good of you to come down and let us know Reece," Mam said as she sat down with them.

"I can give you a lift up if you want to go and see him and maybe we can have a pint on the way back. It is Christmas eve after all."

"Thanks Reece." Dad looked across the room at my mother and asked if she minded if he popped up to see his Dad. "Of course not. I have plenty to do, you go and see him, but don't come home too late."

Dad bent down and picked me up. "Be a good boy for Mam Brian, and I hope to see you later."

"Alright Dad, I'm going to help Mam with making the mince pies, she said I could."

Reece caught hold up me and held me up high into the air. "He's always a good boy, aren't you Bottle?! See you tomorrow."

Dad left with Reece and I waved to them both on the doorstep and watched the van climb the hill until it had disappeared from sight.

That evening, I helped Mam make the mince pies and bake the Christmas cake and then she wrapped Dad's present which I was sure was a shaving set with soap. I sat and waited for Dad to return home. "It's getting late, Brian. You'd better have your bath now. I've started to boil the water and you look like you are about to fall asleep. I'll just put these mince pies on the plate to cool off and you can have one if you like, after your bath."

"Yes please Mam, but make sure we leave two for Father Christmas as he is sure to get hungry on his travels."

"I'll leave them on a plate next to your stocking as he won't miss them there."

She came in from outdoors with a very large enamel bowl that was full of warm water. There was a tablet of green soap floating around and Mam placed it right in front of the warm fireplace.

"You can have a wash down in this tonight. I won't get the big bath out as you're not too dirty."

I took off my clothes and stood up in the bowl while Mam helped me wash my hair. She then wrapped me in a large soft towel and helped me into my clean pyjamas. I sat down by the fire and began eating my mince pie, as I held my stocking in my hand and wondered what I would find inside in the morning. When I had finished eating my treat, Mam helped me hang my stocking above the fireplace. The warm glow of the fire, the smell of the cooking and the excitement I felt inside has stayed with me. This was truly my first memory of Christmas and would be repeated for many more to come. My feelings were full of anticipation and wonder and my innocent young mind told me that I was sure Father Christmas would be visiting me on this special night. Mam followed me as I climbed the stairs to bed. It was dark with only a shaft of light coming in from the living room up the stairway. "Leave the door open for me, Mam, for the light to come through and please wake me when Dad comes home."

"We'll see, your Dad is late though. Goodnight, Brian."

I cuddled Blackie and Ted under the blankets and wondered why Dad wasn't home and I also wondered what gifts I was having for Christmas.

As Christmas morning arrived, I awoke to find a small table beside my bed and on it stood a fire engine, a box of dinky cars and some books. I rubbed my eyes as I was not quite awake and in excitement I ran into Mam's bedroom calling out "He's been! He's been, Father Christmas has been!", but no one was there. I knew it was very early and expected Mam and Dad to be sound asleep. Instead, they were downstairs having tea. "Dad, where were you last night? I was waiting for you and you were so long."

"I'll tell you later," he answered with tears in his eyes. He scooped me up into his arms and said "Let's go and see what Santa has left you first."

We went upstairs and collected my toys and brought them down. "Look Dad, they are great toys and I love this fire engine. Mam, my stocking is hanging from the mantelpiece and it looks full of things!" She took it down and gave it to me and I started to empty it, pulling out small items like paper hats and toy soldiers.

"He ate the mince pies then, did he Mam?"

"Yes, of course he did!" she answered. "I'll get some tea and toast going, your Dad must be hungry."

"Why Mam, When did he get home from granddad Jenkins'?"

"Oh not till late."

"Is Granddad better Dad?" Dad didn't answer. We have a present..

"Have you?" she smiled. "Well go on then, go and get it, I know you can't wait," said Dad. Dad reached high up to the shelf of the pantry to reach the present we had chosen with care for Mam. He passed it to me and I walked over with it in my arms. "It's of us. Dad and I picked it from the market."

"Brian, you're not supposed to tell where it's from when it's a present! Sorry I didn't wrap it properly Urs, as you know, I didn't have time yesterday evening what with going up to Penygarn to see my father."

"Don't worry, I understand," she answered.

Mam opened her present, took the clock out of the wrapping paper and placed it on the mantelpiece above the fireplace. She stood back and looked at it looking very pleased. We sat down and had breakfast together, and then Dad played with me and my new Christmas toys while Mam prepared our Christmas dinner. I was so happy enjoying Christmas with my family in our own home. The aroma of dinner began to fill the house and soon enough it was time to enjoy our festive food. When dinner was finished, Dad said that he had to go to Penygarn to Granddad Jenkins' house.

"Why Dad? Its Christmas day and I want you to stop with me and Mam."

He picked me up and held me close while he cuddled me on his lap. I could sense that something was wrong and that he was unhappy.

"I have something to tell you," he said, as tears welled in his eyes.

"Granddad Jenkins died early this Christmas morning and he's gone up to heaven. I'm so sorry I didn't come home last night to see you go to bed on Christmas Eve. I had to stay up there until early this morning and you were fast asleep when I came home." Tears fell from his eyes and travelled down his cheeks. I put my arms around his neck and hugged him tight, hoping it would make him feel a little better. "Please don't cry Dad, you have me and Mam."

Poor Dad, he was just twenty eight years old and had lost his mother, father and daughter in such a short time.

It was such a sad time for the family, especially for Aunty Iris as she was only thirteen years old. We had all been looking forward to New Year's Day as we had such high hopes for 1946, the first New Year since the end of the war.

A few days later, Dad took me up to Penygarn and as usual, we went in around the back of the house and into the kitchen. Most of the family were there, assembled on chairs around the table. Aunty Iris, Joyce and Emily sat together talking quietly, almost whispering. Dad said that Granddad was lying in the front room. Ted sat in Granddad's old chair looking very forlorn and distant. How strange to think of the happiness that filled this house just a week ago when he returned from the army.

"Can I go and see Granddad in the front room?" I enquired.

"If you want to, but not for long," Dad replied.

I opened the door slowly and spotted a long wooden box with shiny silver handles at the side, and it was standing on two trestles. I pulled a chair close to the coffin and stood upon it, peering over the side to see my granddad. I thought that he looked as if he were asleep and might wake any second, and as I touched his face, it felt very cold. His prominent bald head and white moustache looked like marble. This was the first time I had seen anyone dead and I knew now that he was sleeping and he would never wake up. I turned to Dad and he said that Aunty Joyce had made some tea and cakes and that now I had seen Granddad, I had better go back to the kitchen. I said "Why don't you put Granddad by the fire in the kitchen so that he can go up to heaven nice and warm?"

"We will tomorrow Brian, when he goes to heaven at Trevethin church," replied Aunty Margaret.

"Alright Aunty," I answered as I sat eating my Christmas cake and wondering where exactly heaven was.

The day of the funeral arrived. It was the 29th of December and we went up to Penygarn. John and Margaret were there and the three of us stayed upstairs. Sitting on the top step leading to the landing, we sat and listened to a man dressed in a long black dress with a white collar. He stood next to Granddad's coffin and read from a book and told everyone that Granddad had been a good man and that he was going to meet a man named Paul, as well as Jesus. He said he was going to a better place and that heaven was much nicer than earth. The man also said that Granddad didn't have to work selling fruit and vegetables anymore. John asked me where heaven was and I said I didn't know, but it must be quite near Pontypool. I also told him that I had heard of Jesus because I say my prayers to him every night, but I had never heard of anyone called Paul.

After the vicar or minister, or whoever we thought he was, had finished talking which was a tradition in the Welsh valleys' we went into the front bedroom, lifted the window and began to look out. On the front garden and the pavement and out on the road stood hundreds of men in black suits with most of them wearing Bowler hats. Some stood surrounding a long shiny black van that had windows along the side of it, while two other men stood at the front with tall black hats. There was another shiny black car parked behind. A sudden silence fell upon the street as the front door opened. We stretched our necks to look down over the window sill, being careful not to make a sound.

The coffin appeared, carried by four men who were also dressed in black suits. We could see a large silver plate with writing on it, placed on top of the coffin. As the sun shone down on it, it caught the reflection, and made for an eerie sight indeed. Many carried flowers and wreaths and even though I didn't understand at the time, these locals were proud to show their respects to a man who had given much to the local community. They slid Granddad into the back of the vehicle and covered him with the flowers and wreaths, then they closed the back window and everyone stood still. Dad and his brothers and the men of the family came out. These included Uncles, Ted, and Reece, and, Aunty Margaret's Husband, Frank Beer and Aunt Emily's husband, Eddie Rowland. They walked slowly towards the car and got in without saying a word. The vehicles moved slowly up the road on their journey towards Trevethin church, with hundreds following behind on foot. It seemed like a huge black mist moving past, dotted with white spots from the stiff white collars. It slowly disappeared around the corner. Granddad would be buried in the same grave as my grandmother Jane, next to my sister's grave.

My grandfather, George Jenkins had been a well known man in the Pontypool area. He sold fruit and vegetables from the back of his house in Penygarn from the 'Shed'. He also had a horse and cart from which he sold his produce, and on which he would travel around the local areas. He would travel to the market towns of Usk and Abergavenny to buy the goods and sell it around the roads of Pontypool. 'George Jenks' as he was known, was a popular figure with his long moustache and large round straw hat with black band around it. Whenever we visited Penygarn , I would find Granddad's hat, put it on and march around with his walking stick. I would wave to everyone who came out of the house running after me. "Leave the little lad alone, he won't hurt. We haven't seen him for ages," he would say. Sadly, his death came too soon for him to love me for long, on that sad ending to 1945.

Uncle Ted, the oldest, now became head of the family. As he wasn't sure what job he would undertake, it seemed fitting that he could now take over the fruit and veg business that Granddad had built up. He began to sell from the 'Shed' and soon, Uncle Reece got him a used Austin van for him to collect produce from the country. He mainly used Cliff Howe's farm at Chain Bridge near Usk and he started a 'round' selling from his van around the local roads. Ted was able to drive from his time driving vehicles in the army.

Uncle Ted was a strange man and not that likeable. He always used to moan to John and me about leaving the lights on, but we still loved to stay at Penygarn. He never drank alcohol in his life and he was always coughing as he smoked Woodbine cigarettes continually during the day. He never had any women or men friends and never once visited a doctor or bank. He kept his money and important documents in a large black steel container which was always locked and kept under his bed. Nobody ever saw what was inside. The 'till' in the shed, where the change was kept consisted of a ladies red handbag that used to belong to my grandmother. This was brought into the house every evening and taken upstairs with him each night.

He not only sold fruit and veg, but anything in a tin, Vile Brothers lemonade and Smiths crisps. He went around the roads four days a week and also went up to a small village on top of a mountain called Pantygasseg, or The Pant for short. After he finished his 'round', he emptied his van of the left-over goods and placed them in the 'shed'. The rest of the time he sat in the house and when the back door was knocked, he got up, went to the 'shed' and served. The busiest time was a Sunday morning, and no one was served after 10 o'clock at night.

Dad's younger brother Reece was a different person altogether. He also never married or had any lady friends, neither did he ever go to the doctors or visit a bank, but that's where their similarities ended. He was a loveable character that everyone liked, despite him not being able to read or write and being partially deaf. He returned from Coventry after working in a factory during the war. He was a motor fitter producing vehicles and when he came home to Wales, he worked as a mechanic for Norman Jenkins.(no relation) who had garage business, petrol pumps and car showrooms that were situated on the left as you entered Clarence Street. Norman, his wife and two boys, John and Richard, lived next to the petrol pumps in a house called Weighbridge House. They used an old Blacksmiths shop at the bottom of Mill Road for their repair shop and this is where Reece worked. The workshop was large but very dark, dreary and cold. The only heating came from a coal fired black cast iron stove that stood against the wall. It had small benches on each side for sitting on and everyone was welcome to come in and have a warm. That is if they were prepared to make Uncle Reece a pot of tea. The kettle stood on top of the stove and it boiled continuously. Each time I walked over to visit Uncle Reece, one or more of the Trinder boys would be sat there wearing their wellies, enjoying the warmth of the fire. "Just made a cup of 'Golden' for you, Bri." I don't know why, but Reece always called tea 'Golden'.

Aged 10

On regular visits, I would go over to the workshop and say "It's my birthday today Uncle Reece." He would always laugh saying "You are the only one, Bottle, who has a birthday every month on the 6th. Tell you what, make me a cup of 'Golden' and I'll give you something nice." He always gave me a three penny piece or a sixpence to buy sweets from Bennett's shop. When it was my real birthday, he always gave me two shillings or half a crown. I thought he was great, and I loved it when he came to our house to have dinner with us.

Every evening without fail, Reece would walk down to Pontypool from Penygarn. He would go into one of the local pubs and sit and chat to everyone. He would always finish up at the bar in the Clarence Hotel socialising with the other regulars. Everyone knew and liked him and he had many good friends. The last Peake's bus always left the bus stop outside the hotel at ten thirty. The driver would sound his horn as he pulled up outside and his friends would say "Horn's going, Reece, your bus is waiting" as he was hard of hearing. He would finish his pint bidding everyone goodbye, run outside and jump onto 'his' bus that took him home to Penygarn.

I settled back into school after the Christmas and New Year holidays and life remained about the same for the following year. Times were happy and settled with my mother taking me into town to do the shopping, bathing in front of the fire in the large tin bath before bedtime and waiting for Dad to come home from the mines. I loved to help him fill his bath with water in the outhouse, where he would wash when he came home, as he was always covered in coal dust. I enjoyed my routine of going to school with Michael and playing down the road with the Trinder boys and Terry Relf, Dave Phillips and Tony Guest. We would play cricket, football or 'cowboys and Indians' down the 'wood' which was at the other side of the gasworks. All the families were quite poor and we looked an impoverished sight with patched trousers, holes in our socks and those who didn't have holes were often darned. Those who wore shoes mostly had holes in the soles and we used to put cardboard inside to cover the holes in the bottom.

Mr Trinder always seemed to organise activities for us. He was a thin man who always wore an old grey suit which was too large for him. He displayed no teeth and his mousy hair was combed tightly back and when it dried, it stuck out from the back. This gave the impression that the wind was blowing in his face all of the time. He was a jolly friendly man and could run very fast. He would challenge anyone to a race up around the Clarence and back. Sometimes, his sons or some of the locals would take up the challenge, but he always won. He was confident and fun loving and I always enjoyed his company.

A few things made me despair in my childhood as I progressed to different classrooms with age. At the beginning of each new term, the new teacher would at first seem to be pleasant towards me. They would ask everyone where they came from. "And where do you live, Brian?" they would ask in a pleasing manner. "Mill Road, Miss, down behind the Clarence Hotel," I always answered despairingly. "Isn't that Trosnant?" they would ask, with a sign of humiliation in their voice. "No Miss. Mill Road near the top of Trosnant" I would answer in earnest. They would then dismiss the subject with aloofness as if I wasn't telling the truth. After they discovered where I came from, they never acted the same with me. All the other children in class were called by their first name but when it came to me, I was always referred to as 'Jenkins'.

Even the Headmaster, Mr Griffiths was the same. Each time he spoke to me, it was 'Jenkins'. Even so, I remained respectful to everyone in school making sure I never attracted undue attention and never getting myself into trouble. The only teacher that I liked and who was nice to me was the history teacher, Mr Lewis. He lived at Usk Road and his daughter Pat was in my class. Although the teachers were not kind to me, the children in my class were great, especially the boys, Kenny Blake, Graham Young, Terry Hallet, Billy Walker and Roy Lewis, to name just a few. As my birthday was in August, I was the youngest class member.

Being the only child at the time, my mother would take me to the cinema and we often went about two evenings each week. It was a wonderful experience going to The Royal, The Park Cinema and the Pavilion which was the best one. We had to travel on Peake's bus to Pontnewynydd to go there, which wasn't far from Granddad Jones' house. We always bought Payne's Poppets, which were round chocolates in a box, or Plush Nuggets.

As we still had no electricity in the house, it was silent coming home. It was such a different atmosphere from the exciting hustle bustle of the cinemas we had visited. In the winter, it was bitterly cold going to bed. My bedroom window was loose and rattled as the wind blew and the rain pounded the glass. In the depths of winter, ice would appear at my window and I would cling to my faithful toys, Ted and Blackie, keeping as warm as I could under the blankets.

The winter of 1947 was particularly harsh. There was a heavy snow fall that drifted high up to the window sill of my bedroom. All the men on Mill Road dug a pathway up the centre of the road and to each of the houses.

When you came out from your front door, the snow towered ten feet high, and inside our houses, it was dark as night as the snow did not let any light in from the windows. Dad managed to dig a gap in the snow from the back door to the outhouse and the toilet.

The houses in the area were in a poor state and no electricity made life in winter very difficult. We had very little in the way of possessions and very much lived 'hand to mouth'. Often cold and dressed in poor clothing, we struggled through this time. The day the snow came made everything sparkle. The old houses took on a different look; the trees were covered in what reminded me of pure white puffs of cotton wool. Nature was hard on us, but at the same time it brought such beauty to us. We had great fun sliding up and down the road, playing snow ball fights and building snow men. Sometimes good comes from hard situations and the children from Mill Road made the most from the short time the snow remained. As the day drew to a close, I shivered as I made my way home. I noticed the stillness of the air and felt a tingly feeling as the light breeze caused a small sprinkling of snow to fall from the bare branches of a tree. Everything seemed to glisten in the fading light and the heavy clouds took on a colour that was not usual to them, a slightly orange pink shade. As I made my way into the house where my mother and father waited for me, I silently wished that the clouds above held more snow, which would fall overnight while I slept.

Chapter 6

Jennifer

During the latter years of 1948, as Dad sat close to the fire one evening, he began talking to my mother and me about his plans for the future. He began to speak about starting his own fruit and vegetable round. He was familiar with this as he used to have his own fruit stall in Pontypool Market, as a young man before the war.

"I think I'd like to start my own fruit round, Urs. I hate it in the coal mines and it's so dirty. The coal dust is beginning to affect my chest and I've a job to breathe sometimes."

"Yes, I know you have a bad chest," Mam answered. "It's alright by me if you could get out of the mines. But what would you use? You can't drive."

"I could use a horse and cart like my father used years ago. A friend of mine has a horse for sale for a few pounds up at a place called 'The Race'. I could keep it in his field where there's a stable. We'll have to take the horse back there every night though."

"That's alright Dad, I will come with you," I said excitedly.

"I can use the cart my father used. It's still kept in the shed in the field our Ted rents at Penygarn. I saw it there a few weeks ago and it's still in pretty good condition."

I listened intently. I didn't like Dad going down the mines and coming home covered in coal dust.

"Can I come with you on the cart, Dad? I can help you when I'm not in school. I can go and knock on people's doors and feed the horse. Could I have a ride on it?"

"Of course you can, son," Dad said, as if it was definite that he was going to go ahead with his plan.

"If the three of us pull together, I'm sure things will work out ok. I'm going to be a greengrocer, I hope!" he said with a smile.

"I hope you know what you're doing," Mam spoke, with a sign of apprehension.

I went to bed that night and snuggled under the blankets telling Ted and Blackie that Dad wasn't going down the mines much longer.

A few days later, I looked out of the window and glanced over to where the tip began. On a small area of grass, close to this stood a cart. Reece had towed it from the field at Penygarn. It was my grandfather's old cart that Dad had spoken about.

The cart was flat and made of wood, with a head board running along the front. It had large wooden wheels on each side and two long shafts at the front where the horse stood and pulled it along. It looked very old and rather worn out with quite a bit of paint peeling off it. It was badly in need of some tender loving care and I knew that Dad was just the man for the job. I glanced at it and began to wonder where I was going to sit when it was full of crates of fruit and vegetables.

Aged 12 outside no. 14 Mill Road

The following weekend I started helping Dad to rub down the woodwork. This had to be done before Mam could help us with the painting of the headboard and sides of the cart. They were to be green and the wheels were going to be red. Dad never did any painting as Mam said he was hopeless at it. She never gave Dad any praise about anything he did. Even at my young age, I was conscious of this. When the painting had been completed, it looked very smart standing opposite our house. We stared at it with a look of satisfaction etched upon our faces and Dad said that his father would have been proud of it. "Well, the cart's ready now, so I guess it's time to buy the horse. First I've got to go and make sure about a small warehouse I'll need. The owner of the Hanbury public house at the top of the Trosnant has a small one on the side of the pub that would be ideal and he said I could rent it," Dad said to us that evening.

After breakfast on Sunday morning, Dad said he was taking me with him to collect the horse and bring it to the cart to see how she got on with it. We walked to a place called 'The Race,' which was about a mile away from Mill Road, on top of a large hill called Blaendare. We came upon a field at the side of the road and a man's voice called out "Aubrey, I'm over here." The voice came from a man sat on an old wooden bench outside a small stone built stable with a corrugated tin roof. We opened the gate and walked across to him. "Hello Coco," said Dad as he shook his hand. "Alright Aub? Come for Jennifer have you? This is your boy Brian, isn't it? Damn, he is growing up. How old is he now?" he said, smiling down at me. "Eight in August, Coco," Dad replied.

I stood there, looking at this strange looking man, opening the stable door. He had a long grey beard and wore a grey cap. He was badly stooped over and was using a walking stick which he obviously relied heavily upon. I thought to myself what a silly name to have. Then I guessed that Coco had to be a nickname that he probably got stuck with from when he was a boy. Then I recalled him calling the horse Jennifer so it must be a female. Not that I could tell the difference, of course. The man led the horse out of the stable and gave the reins to Dad. I looked up at her head and could just about smooth her nose. Jennifer seemed so big. I had expected a much smaller horse. I glanced at her and at once, I knew that I loved her. She was chestnut brown with a white forehead and white ankles. I knew that she and I were going to be very special to each other.

"She's getting on a bit, Aub, but she is strong and has many years left in her. She's very gentle with kids around her and safe on the road. I've had her a fair few years working on my farm, but now I am giving it all up. I'm still going to keep some pigs though. Tell you what, you can have Jenny for nothing if you promise to look after her," he said as he stroked her mane. "And you can keep her in this field as well if you like. Your Dad George was a good friend of mine years ago. Just bring me up all your waste fruit and veg you don't want and I can feed it to my pigs. They will eat anything."

"Thanks, Coco. I don't know your real name, I only know Coco!" He immediately put his hand up to stop Dad talking. "Don't worry Aub, everybody calls me that, besides, I forget my real name sometimes, bin called that all my life, too late to change now, ay?"

"We'll look after her. You can see her every evening and I'll only use her four days a week. I won't work her hard and she'll be standing more than pulling the cart along," Dad said, as he patted Jennifer's neck.

Coco went into the stable and came out with a pile of leather straps. "Here Aub, you can have this bridle and reins, as I don't think I will be needing them anymore." He placed the big round padded object over Jennifer's head so it sat around the bottom of her neck. "Now that's the bridle. You connect this to the cart shafts so that she can pull the cart along. Now this is the 'bit'. This metal bar comes across the inside of her mouth and connects to the reins with these straps that come around her head to keep it all together."

Coco then pointed his stick at Dad and said "Let me give you some tips. When you get going on the road, always have the reins in your hands, sit on the cart on the pavement side at the front as it's safer. Now, when you want to move off, jerk up the reins high, so they come down on her back. Don't worry, it won't hurt her, give a loud tu tut through your teeth at the same time and she will slowly pull away. When you want to turn left, make a tu tu noise and pull the left rein hard. This will pull the 'bit' in her mouth and she will know which way you want to turn. The same with the right turn and when you want to stop pull hard on both reins and shout 'woe' loudly. Always give her plenty of time to stop. She will get used to you in no time. When you walk along the road, always hold her reins near to her head as she won't be afraid then. She'll know that you're near her. She has been fed this morning and there's plenty of hay in the barn you can use. I'll be here later to see how you got on with her and then I'll tell you about feeding her. Alright, Aub, off you go.

Coco then pulled the straps by her head and handed it to Dad. He then started walking proudly across the field with her. He shook hands with Coco and thanked him for everything. He said he would see him later and we began walking back home together. Jen was no trouble and Dad was so proud when people he knew stopped us in the street to ask who Jen belonged to. "She is ours. I am going to start a fruit and veg round with her." Everyone wished Dad the best of luck.

When we arrived home, Dad tied Jen between the shafts of the cart that stood opposite our house. Mam came out to see her and was surprised at how big she was. "Mam, what do you think her name is? It's Jennifer!" I said, before she could answer. "Really, that's a nice name for a horse!" Mam replied. "The man Dad had her off calls her Jenny sometimes and he had a funny name. Dad called him Coco."

As we stood there, some of the people came out from their houses to take a look at Jennifer. She caused quite a stir on Mill Road. "Fine horse you've got there, Aub. I think the breed they call them is a Welsh Cob," said Mr Ford. Then Mr Smith next door up came out, held an apple in his flat hand and gave it to Jenny to eat. "We haven't seen a horse down here since your old man George had one years ago," he said to Dad.

By now, Jennifer was surrounded by people of all ages who were making a fuss of her. Billy Trinder offered to take her back to the field every evening for Dad.

Bill loved horses and was in awe of her. "We'll see, Bill. Let her get used to us all first," Dad answered. "Now all stand back. I want her to get used to the cart," he told everyone. Dad caught hold of the strap near her ears and started walking down the road. Jenny followed him holding the cart steadily. They turned around at the bottom of the road and Dad then walked all the way to the top of Mill Road and back down again, just for Jenny to get used to him and her new surroundings. Mam had cooked our Sunday dinner by now, and she called out to me and Dad. We sat at the table having our dinner and wondered what to do next. Mam said "Why don't the two of you go for a practice ride pulling the cart? You should go when it's empty first, for her to get the feel of it before you go out loaded with goods. It'll be good for Jennifer to go empty first."

"Yes I think we'll go after dinner. You ready, Bri?"

"Yes Dad, I'd love to," I answered, not quite knowing what to expect when I got onto the cart.

When we were ready, we went outside and patted Jen first. We walked to the bottom of the road, turned the cart around and faced up Mill Road. Dad lifted me onto the side then he got on and sat in front leaning over the headboard. I tucked in tight to Dad, catching hold of his belt around his waist. "Hold tight. Are you ready?" "Yes I am, Dad," I replied. Dad jerked the reins up high until they came down on Jen's back. He said a loud tut tut through his teeth and Jenny started to trot forward. Up Mill Road we travelled, while some of the neighbours waved good luck to us. Dad pulled on the reins and called out a loud woe noise to get her to stop at the top of

Trosnant. "You alright son?" Dad asked as he glanced down at me. "Yes, no problem, It's a bit shaky, but it's alright," I answered.

"We'll turn left here, go up to the Clarence, turn left again and carry on down towards Pontymoile, then head back home again."

"Yes carry on, it's great Dad," I said, still clinging onto his belt. We came back home and parked Jen and the cart opposite our house. Mam came out, as did some of the neighbours, to see if everything had gone well. "You both alright?" Mam asked. "Yes, everything's fine. A bit bumpy but pleased with our trip. Jennifer did everything I wanted her to do," Dad answered, as he patted her back. "Make us a cup of tea, Urs, and then I'll take Jenny back up the field and feed her." Later, Dad walked Jenny back up to the field and Billy Trinder went with him.

That evening, as Dad sat and talked about his next move, thoughts turned to how he was going to begin his fruit and veg round, delivering to houses in the area.

Ted came to our house the next day and discussed with Dad the ways he could help him. Ted was happy to travel to the country farms and collect the goods in his van to help Dad start up his round. I don't think Dad could have done it without Ted's help in the beginning. The plan was that the following Thursday they were going to collect sacks of potatoes and crates of fruit and vegetables from the farms and store it in the warehouse that Dad had rented at the top of Trosnant. Friday morning, Dad would collect Jenny from the field, connect her to the cart, and then take her up to the warehouse where he would load the cart with goods. He would then travel to the houses in the area of Trosnant and Pontymoile, knocking on doors and asking if anyone would like to purchase any fruit or veg. Dad planned to call twice a week if anyone was interested. Dad would then return Jenny to the field in the evening and carry out the same system the next day if he had enough stock in the warehouse.

That week, Dad gave up his job at the coal mines and was so relieved to know that maybe he would never have to go down a mine again. At the same time, this was such a big venture for Dad, and he was unsure if the future would be bright for us. Having his own business as a greengrocer was a big move for him.

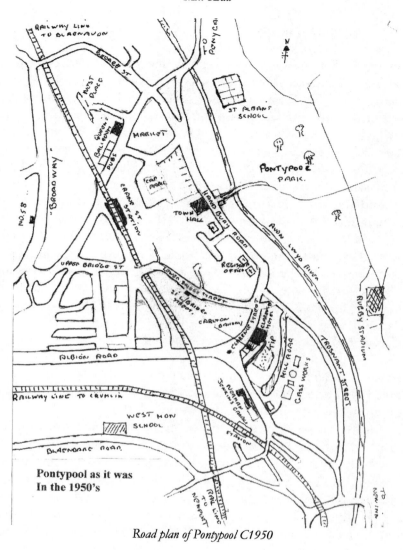

Road plan of Pontypool C1950

The start of the business turned out well for Dad. With the help of Uncle Ted, he began to build up two rounds. One on a Tuesday, and Friday, and a different round on a Wednesday and Saturday. Monday and Thursday were his buying days where he travelled to the farms. Wholesalers would also call with their vans. On a Sunday, he cleaned the warehouse and got rid of the waste and rubbish, and cleaned Jen and her stable as well. Dad was a hard working man, but times were difficult and profit was hard to make as people would not pay any more for their groceries than what they were on sale for in the market. Sometimes, he even lost money as the fruit and veg would decay early before he managed to sell it.

It was expensive for Dad to have new metal shoes fitted to Jennifer's hoofs as she wore them down very quickly, trotting around the roads. I loved going to the blacksmiths shop with Dad to have her shoes fitted. I used to sit next to the fire and pump the bellows for the blacksmith who was called Mr Jackson. He was a short man with a balding head with a few stray black hairs that he combed over the top of his head. He had a short black moustache and was slightly cross eyed. He reminded me of Groucho Marks and had massive strong arms from lifting his sledge hammer to shape the shoes around the anvil. His muscles would bulge each time he swung the hammer high into the air. It would come crashing down shaping the shoes as it landed upon the anvil. "Pump up the bellows lad, keep the fire going," he would yell. I watched him make the horse shoes for Jen while she stood motionless nearby. He had a large pair of leather bellows that were inserted into a crevice on the side of the furnace. I pumped until my arms ached. After the new shoes were made, he would take the old ones off Jen, file her hoofs flat and then nail the new shoes on. I enjoyed the experience and looked forward to seeing Mr Jackson at his work.

There was a small lean-to building attached to the blacksmiths shop where a man called Mr Stevens worked. He chopped and sold firewood for a living. He was a little weedy man who always wore a cloth cap. He had slanty eyes and large bushy eyebrows. I used to peer through a small crack in the door and watch him as he sat upon a wooden stool. In front of him stood a large round block of very hard wood and to his left was a pile of wood blocks. He placed these in front of him with his left hand and would strike it at least ten times with a very sharp axe. Around twenty pieces would then be wrapped tight into a bundle with a short length of wire from a pile he kept to his right. This sight amazed me as he carried out this task in around twenty seconds flat. He then threw the bundle onto a pile which was ready to go into sacks, which he then sold around the houses. Over the years, I think he must have missed a few times as he had his left thumb missing and half of his forefinger was gone. The whole building is now a motor cycle business, run by Ray Coles who was renowned for tuning and setting up motorcycles in the racing world.

When I wasn't at school, I used to help Dad on his 'rounds'. I would sit tight behind him and hold onto his waist as we travelled along the roads. It was a long working day as we had to pick Jennifer up early in the morning and work all day loading the cart with goods, travelling around selling them, only to take her back up to the field late in the evening and make sure she was fed before heading home.

On a fine warm day, it was a joyful task, but when it rained, I had to wear a black plastic hat shaped like a cowboy hat and a black plastic mackintosh. Winter was hard. I didn't like the cold weather or the snow and I used to enjoy going into people's homes or public houses, to warm myself by their fires. The problem with the cart was that it had no roof and so we had no shelter from the rain. Many times we came home soaked through to the skin and the fruit and veg became very wet if we could not cover it quick enough with a plastic sheet.

It was my job to knock on the doors of the houses and I would weigh the potatoes. When a regular customer was not at home, I would leave some potatoes and vegetables at the rear of their homes. Dad never left anyone without. Most of Dad's customers who had their goods in the week would put it on Dad's 'slate book,' then on the weekends, they would pay for goods received for both days. Unless of course they had a hard luck story and were unable to pay. Dad was a soft touch to when it came to times like that. He was soft and kind hearted and many took advantage of his generosity. When his working day was over, he returned home late in the evening and sometimes during the harder winter months, the evenings would become bitterly cold. He came home to Mam expecting a warm welcome but unfortunately, she never seemed to show him much comfort or warmth.

I understood that my mother didn't have an easy life. She found it difficult living in such an old house with just a tap outside and no electricity. The outlook of the tip was also not particularly pleasant and we had very little home comforts. But I also understood that she could have shown love and warmth to Dad as he tried his best for us. Later on, I found that he turned to drink and he started calling into pubs and drinking while he was on his 'round', to drown his sorrows. It was a long progression, but years later, it sadly proved to be his demise.

Chapter 7

Nightmares

A disturbing phase of my life began when I was around seven years old. I started to realise that Mam and Dad's relationship was not that good and they weren't getting on well with each other. This was mainly because Mam was unable to express any warmth towards him, particularly when he returned home late from working. He complained bitterly that she never called him by his name, Aubrey, or show him any love or affection. This would lead to violent rows on many occasions.

Dad, being very emotional, yearned for a kind word or an act of affection like simply her placing her arm around him, but this was never forthcoming. She was always so cold towards him and this made me feel sad. I realised that sometimes being emotional was not an asset, but more a liability.

Each time an argument occurred; I would run out into the darkness of the pantry and cower down in the corner. I would put my hands over my ears to drown out the cruel words being said and would shout 'no, no, please'. I felt scared, lonely and very insecure.

Mam was a good mother though. She always kept Dad and me clean and tidy with a clean shirt to wear each day, and always made sure we had enough to eat, the best she could. But Dad yearned for her to care for him in the ways a wife should care for her husband. He needed her to provide a kind word, a happy smile, a cuddle and some warmth. Sadly, this never came. I knew he did his best for us and although Dad loved me very much, it was Mam's love that he searched for all his life.

The arguments between my parents left a profound mark on my memory of my young days. They told me that they had married in St James Church, but there were no photographs or anything to show me when I asked. One day as I was looking for something in the chest of drawers in the bedroom, I came across their marriage certificate and discovered they had got married in Pontypool Registry Office in July 1940. I became very distressed when I realised that I was born the very next month and it seemed that they had only married because of my imminent birth. I began to feel a huge sense of insecurity at the thought that I had caused them to be together and that I was the sole reason for the marriage. I never spoke a word to either of them about what I had discovered.

They argued sometimes when I had gone to bed. I laid there in the dark holding onto Blackie and Teddy and tried hard not to hear their voices. The flicker of the gas light coming from downstairs cast shadows up the stairway like an evil devil about to climb up to my room. I closed my eyes and wished that I was somewhere else, Aunt Emily's, Aunty Marge's or Grandad's. Anywhere but there.

The turmoil in my mind always led to my dreams becoming nightmares. I would be running and running away from something, only wearing a short dirty shirt that came only to my waist. A classic sign of my insecurity and inability to feel safe. I dreamt of running through town. All the roads were empty but the pavements were crowded with people who were laughing and jeering at me. I would try to run along different roads to get away, but it was always the same story around every corner. Some of the faces appeared larger than others and these belonged to my teachers at school who they would be pointing their fingers at me saying 'Trosnant, Trosnant, he's from Trosnant.' I would try to cover myself over as I ran crying and answering back through my tears saying 'No, no, Mill Road, Mill Road.' As I woke in the morning, I felt relieved to know it was just a dream, and I hoped that one day things would be alright between my mother and father.

By now, Reece had finished working for Norman Jenkins and had started working for himself. He began his own repair business with a small workshop in Penygarn called Hilltop Garage where he repaired cars. He also bought and sold the odd one or two cars. This was a difficult period for Reece as he could hardly read or write.

One evening, he came to our house and spoke to Dad about him using a van to sell his fruit and veg from, instead of using the horse and cart. He knew how hard things were, especially during the dark winter months. "Aubrey, I have a Morris van that I bought very cheap the other day. The body's a little rusty as it was laid up during the war, but the engine is alright. You can have it if you like and pay me so much a week." Dad sat there looking very serious, not knowing quite what to say. Mam said "but he can't drive a motor vehicle."

"Don't worry about that, he doesn't need a licence yet. They are not bringing in the testing until next year and I can start teaching him to drive straight away," Reece answered. With a beam on his face, Dad's eyes lit up behind his dark brown glasses and he thanked Reece for the offer. He said that the van would be so much better than the horse and cart and seemed relieved at the fact that he wouldn't need to walk to the field and back every day. He said he was sure that he would soon be able to drive with some help and tuition from Uncle Reece and Uncle Ted.

Listening to what had been said, I sprang to my feet and spoke to Dad saying "but what's going to happen to Jennifer? I don't want to part with her. I love that horse." Dad looked at me, smiled and put his arms around me and answered "Don't worry, we can still keep her. We can go up to the field and feed and walk her. It's about time she retired anyway. She has worked hard and Coco said to me the other day that we could keep her, even if we retired her. He knew we would look after her."

"I suppose it will be alright then. I expect she's getting old now and she could do with a rest. Billy and I can go up to the field and feed her after school."

The next day, Reece brought 'Dad's new van' down from Penygarn and parked it opposite our house. It was a scruffy dark brown Morris Commercial. I knew this because I read the name on the chrome badge set inside the radiator cover. Dad sat in the driver's seat and played with the gear lever. Mam sat next to him in the passenger seat, winding the windows up and down. "This will be much better, Brian," Dad said to me through the open window. "It will be so much warmer in here than sat on the open cart."

"I know, but I'll miss Jen when I come out with you on the weekends," I answered. "Now stop worrying and don't forget, we can drive up to the field to see her in this van. We won't have to walk all the way up the Race Hill any more."

"Ok Dad, I won't think about it any more as long as you promise that we can see her as often as we like." Dad smiled reassuringly and I knew he would keep his word.

The Relf family had left 16 Mill Road and had gone to live at Trevethin. Bill Morgan and his family had now moved into the house. Bill Morgan and Mr Trinder strolled up the road to look at the van and Dad started talking to them both about painting and altering the van for the fruit and veg to be more accessible to serve people. They both offered to help my father and he was very grateful to them. These were good friends to have and Dad knew he could rely upon them. There was a real sense of community during this time, which really was heart warming. Over the next few days, they helped my father cut the panels away from the sides and remove the rear doors. The driving and passenger seat area was separate from the rear section and they hand painted it a dark green colour. It looked quite good, a big improvement on the mucky brown colour. All I could think about was what if the heater didn't work! I looked forward to travelling in the warmth.

The first Sunday after the van was finished, Reece came down to our house to take Dad out for his first driving lesson. They went out into the countryside and after a few hours, they returned with Dad driving down Mill Road and turning at the bottom. Mam and I ran out to greet them. We were very pleased to actually see my father driving. "He's doing very well," said Reece. "A few more hours and he'll be able to go out on his own."
"It's much easier than I thought, Urs," Dad said to Mam. "The roads are quiet today but I don't think I'll have too much trouble though next week."
"Well done you two! I've got the kettle on and you both deserve a cup of tea," Mam said happily. We strolled back up to the house, past the Trinders and the Morgan's who came out to see how Dad was getting on with his driving. Dad said that he was doing very well, and he thanked them again for the help they had given him in painting and altering the van. Dad turned around and looked back at where the van was parked at the bottom of the road. "She looks great. I can't wait to start my rounds with my 'new van'. It will be much easier for me next week," he spoke, almost to himself. The following Tuesday before I went to school, Dad got ready for work and kissed us both good morning. He walked out of the house proudly towards his new van parked opposite our house. He sat in the driving seat and began to drive slowly down Mill Road, turning at the bottom before driving back up the hill. As he passed us, he waved and we waved back at him from the doorstep. "Dad's a good driver, isn't he Mam?" I said. "Yes he seems to be. I hope he'll be ok," she replied, with a slightly worried look on her face.

That evening after school, my mother and I waited for my father to come home. We listened eagerly for the sound of the engine from the van coming down the road. Just then, the van came into sight from around the corner with Dad driving slowly. He wore a big smile and his eyes lit up from behind his glasses. We rushed out and gave him a huge hug, as we were so relieved to see him home safe and sound. It had been a big day for him, his first day out driving on his own. We were all very proud. After tea, Dad suggested that we went up to the field to feed Jennifer. I was very pleased with this and looked forward to my first ride in the van. Mam came with us and I sat in the middle of the two of them. We headed up to the field, just the three of us and we all felt very excited and happy as we enjoyed the journey together.

It is now August 1948 and I was 8 years old. My birthday present was a new wooden wheelbarrow painted green. Aunty Marge still came down to our house to do her washing on a Monday, and she and Mam kept each other company carrying out the chores in our back yard. When I came home from school, I helped her by putting the bags of washing into my barrow and pushing it up Mill Road to her house. Michael and I would usually have tea there together.

A few weeks before Christmas, my father had received some good news in the post from the gas board, informing him that they were about to fit a new gas fire in the room and would be taking away the old coal fireplace. In addition, the electric board would be installing electric into the house, which was very exciting for us all. Mam especially thought the news was fantastic, for it would make such a difference to her in particular. She thought it was great that there would be no more black coal being carried through the house in the old buckets that she used. With the huge coal fire gone, she would have more room in the house and the outhouse, as she would not need to store coal in there. We all hoped that we would have gas and electric before Christmas came. I thought to myself that we could even have a radio which would be great.

Two weeks later, they came to fit the fire and the electric and when I got home from school, I glanced at where the fireplace once stood. Instead, there was a gas fire and it looked so small standing on the floor. The big old space was plastered and filled in and the room looked so light without the big black old thing. By the end of the next day, most of the electric had been fitted and I thought it was wonderful being able to switch on the lights instead of looking around for matches to light the gas. The best part of all was when I went to bed, I could go on my own and put the light on and off in my bedroom. This was very useful as my nightmares continued and if I woke during the dark night, I could put the light on and read a comic until I fell asleep again. I usually read the Dandy or the Beano.

I continued to help my father on his rounds with his van at the weekends and on busy days leading up to Christmas, while I was on school holidays. The van made life so much easier than the cart. We could keep the goods undercover and I could enjoy a warm close to the heater.

Christmas 1948 saw the electric fitting complete and Dad bought a wireless set for us to listen to. Mam had bought a new sideboard and placed it proudly on the top. That evening, we huddled around the new gas fire and listened to the sounds that the wireless sent us. I for one was amazed at the small gadget.

Starting back to school at the beginning of 1949 was a pleasure. In the mornings, I would put the gas fire on and think how lovely it was to be warm. I would place a piece of bread on a toasting fork and hold it in front of the fire until it was ready to eat. I always made the tea and toast for Mam and Dad when he did not have to get up early and go to work. I would listen for the bells that would chime at West Monmouth Grammar School, as they would tell me that it was ten to nine, time for me to leave and head off to Park Terrace School, knocking on the door at number 6 Trosnant, shout for Michael and carry on our journey together up Bridge Street and into school.

Although I was a child at the time, I was aware that money was very hard to come by and I always liked to earn money for myself, especially to go to the pictures. There were three cinemas in Pontypool, two in town called the Royal and the Park cinemas and one at Pontnewynydd called the Pavilion.

I used to collect small items of scrap metal from the tip that was thrown out with peoples' rubbish. I would place it in my wheelbarrow and take it to the scrap metal dealers down at the bottom of Trosnant. Frank Harris had his shed on the right side and his brother, who everyone called 'Rag' Harris, had his yard on the left side. I usually went to Rag Harris, as when he tipped the scrap out to sort it and weigh it, he would give me an extra few pennies so that I could afford to go to the cinema.

One day, when Mam and Dad had gone shopping, I started to collect some scrap metal, but I loaded my wheelbarrow too much. As I struggled to push it up Mill Road, I slipped outside Mrs Phillips' house and my face fell into the jagged metal. A sharp piece cut a deep wound into my chin and blood started spurting out over the metal. I cried with the pain and because I was frightened at what Mam and Dad would say when they got home as they told me to stay indoors. Mrs Phillips came running out. "God, what have you done, Brian?" she said as she held her teacloth tightly against my chin to stop the stem of blood. "I'm sorry, Mrs Phillips but I slipped."

"You shouldn't be doing this, where's your Mam?"

"Gone shopping" I answered sheepily.

Just then, Mrs Trinder came down the road and realised what had happened. "Our Tommy done that the other week, but his cut wasn't as bad as that," she said. "I know Urs and Aubrey are in town. You silly boy, we will have to get you to the doctor," she said as she held back my head. "I'll take him Mrs Phillips, if you like."

"Shall I come too?"

"If you want to, but someone should be here in case his mother comes home."

"Alright, here's another cloth to help stop the bleeding."

Mrs Trinder took me to Doctor Bertram Siddons Surgery on the Clarence opposite the Clarence Hotel. I sat in the surgery, shaking and covered in blood as the doctor and his wife stitched the large cut underneath my chin and covered it with a large plaster.

"Be careful and don't do such a stupid thing again. You could have marked your face for life, and tell your mother to bring you back in a weeks time to have the stitches out," the doctor warned me. "Yes sir, I won't do it again, I promise" I answered and still felt very frightened at what Mam was going to say.

Mrs Trinder then took me home and called at Mrs Phillips' to show that I was all right. She popped her head out of the door and asked how I was. Mrs Trinder said that I was a bit shaky and she asked if Mam had arrived home from her shopping trip. As she wasn't back, I sat in the Trinders' home until she arrived. She placed a large blanket around me and gave me a warm drink. The Trinder boys sat looking at me and wondering if it could happen to them as they very often collected scrap in the wheelbarrows just as I had.

When Mam and Dad came to collect me, they thanked Mrs Trinder for her help. She said it was no trouble and hoped I was feeling better. When we got home I thought I would be put to bed for what had happened, but to my relief, they were ok with me as long as I promised not to do it again.

On my next visit to the doctor, the stitches were removed and the doctor said the scar would take a long time to heal. In fact, the scar remains under my chin to this day, a reminder of a childhood experience that I have never forgotten.

One Sunday afternoon in early February, my father said he was going up to the field to feed Jennifer. I asked if I could go as well, as I had not seen her for a week, Dad said that I could go and help him give her a brush down. I jumped into the van and we headed off up to the field. As we pulled up outside the gate, I expected to see Jen running out as she always did. "That's unusual, I wonder where she is? Perhaps Coco has taken her for a walk." We opened the gate and Dad called out to her. We looked around the field, but there was no sight of her. My father walked towards the stable in the far corner of the field. "I expect she's in here, but she doesn't usually stay inside for long," he said as he shrugged his shoulders. He called out her name as he went inside and I stood and wondered why it seemed so quiet. Dad came out a few moments later, looking pale and sad. "Don't go in, I think Jennifer has died," he said.

"Oh no Dad, please don't say any more, maybe she's just sleeping," I answered, with tears streaming from my eyes.

"I'm afraid it looks like she has died. We'll have to go over to Coco's house and tell him what's happened." We walked to his farmhouse that was not too far away and we found him feeding his pigs.

"Hello Aubrey, how are you? Nice to see you both," he said.

"Not bad Coco, but we just came up to feed Jen and I found her on the stable floor. I think she may have died."

"Oh dear, I'll come over now and have a look at her with you."

We walked back to the field and all the way, I hoped that Jen was just sleeping and that she would come trotting towards us. Coco went inside for a moment and then appeared saying that he thought my father was right. "She's gone," he said, pensively. "She's been quiet lately too. I guess it was her heart and her old age. Jen is about 35 years old now. At least she died peacefully. She was a great horse, wasn't she Aubrey?"

"She really was, Coco. What will I have to do now?" Dad asked, as he stared at the stable. "Don't worry Aub, I will take care of her. I have a few mates living nearby who can help me. We'll most likely bury her in the corner of the field over there," he said pointing towards some bushes in the far corner.

"Thanks very much, it's very good of you to do this do I owe you anything for this?"

"No, not likely. She was my horse as well as yours, Aub and you looked after her as well as you could. You and your boy did a good job and she enjoyed her time with you." He bent forward and ruffled my hair.

"You ok lad?" he said in a quiet voice. "Yes. But I'll miss Jen." I replied.

"We all will." He answered. I then asked if I could see her, before we went home and Dad said I could. He put his arm around me as we entered the stable and I went into the large room with the floor covered in hay. A wide shaft of light came in from a small glass window shattering the darkness inside. At first, I could not see her, and then under the window, close to the wall, she laid still and lifeless. I knelt down beside her and stroked her gold coloured mane. She just seemed as if she was sleeping peacefully. Many memories came flooding back. The times she spent trotting around the roads pulling Dad's cart along and the carrots that I used to feed her when she stood still as Dad served his customers. Thoughts of feeding Jen and walking her around the field filled my mind. I felt happy that I had had the opportunity to spend time with Jen and I hoped that she had enjoyed the time she had spent with us.

Dad called out quietly that he thought it was time to go, as my mother would be worrying. I stroked her for the last time and walked out slowly, looking backward at the dark corner where I had left her.

"Goodbye Jennifer," I managed to say, wiping away the tears from my face.

On our way home, we called into Aunty Marge's house to let them know what had happened. While Dad parked his van opposite our house, I went down the road to tell the Trinder family the sad news. They were very upset, especially Billy, as he was very fond of Jen and used to love to take her up the field and feed her with us.

Chapter 8

Barry Island

As a family, we never had the pleasure of going anywhere on holiday, as Dad worked every day on his rounds to satisfy his customers. I can remember my father taking me on a pleasure trip on one occasion; it was one evening when Derek was in hospital, to Barry Island This was a rather poor seaside town situated around thirty miles away from Pontypool, approximately ten miles from Cardiff. We were lucky enough however, to have a daily trip, twice-yearly to Barry Island, my mother and I, along with Aunty Marge's family would travel on Peake's Buses. Arranged by Mount Pleasant Church Pontypool.

It was always on a Sunday morning and the bus would leave at nine o'clock. Around one hundred parents and excited children, mainly from Mill Road and Trosnant would gather at the bus stop, eagerly waiting for the buses to appear opposite the town hall. Mums and Dads would be carrying bags, laden with towels, blankets and food. Expectations of a happy day at the seaside filled all our heads and there was such a buzz in the air. Children whispered to one another how much pocket money they had to spend on the fairground and for treats at the beach.

Each family had a large ticket with a number one, two or three printed on it and this indicated which bus we were to get on. Everyone leaned forward anticipating the arrival of the busses, looking back at the town centre, and up at the town hall clock to check the time. The instant the clock displayed a minute after nine o'clock, irritable grumbling could be heard quoting 'Peake,s buses are always late.' Then, everyone cheered, as a convoy of buses appeared with each bus displaying large letters 'Barry Island' with its number written across the side of the windscreen. The buses, always painted dark grey with a light grey stripe at one side, had a huge radiator grill that would shake at the front and the sound of the brakes would always squeal as they pulled up against the wooden bus stop barriers. The crowd frantically formed into three separate groups at the steps of each bus, as the drivers descended from their cabs to the front of each bus. Everyone made way as they took up their positions at the steps.

"Tickets please!" they shouted, as everyone came forward. The tickets were clipped, making sure the number printed was for the appropriate bus. After everyone had settled down, the buses pulled away in convoy with huge cheers ringing out.

Barry Island 1952 with Mam, Dad and Susan

The journey took about two hours. When we arrived in Barry, the three buses would park together in the car park behind the railway station, and a discussion would take place around what time we would be returning home. It was always around seven o'clock. A mad rush to the beach would then take place in order that we could purchase one of the deck chairs, as there were never enough for all the families that were about to descend. We would dash as quickly as we could and make sure we got a good spot on the beach, as by the time afternoon arrived, it would be crammed to capacity. Our party would set up the deck chairs in a large circle and put all our belongings such as buckets and spades, and bags with all our towels and food and drinks, the men then put handkerchiefs over their heads and the women headscarves to shield from the sun. We spent most of the day here, enjoying the food that we brought along, splashing around in the sea and building sand castles. The final hour before returning to the bus was spent at the fair ground. The ghost Train was always my favourite, the highlight of the afternoon was buying Candy floss, the soft pink stuff fascinated me, as it disappeared in my mouth. We had great fun before our pocket money ran out.

I look back at these days with very fond memories. It seems now that these days were filled with wonder and awe, for we had so little, but we made the most of what we had. The seaside was such an exciting place to visit. Even though the sea was cold and it took what seemed ages to reach the shoreline, we had such fun splashing around in the waves. We would spend hours playing in the sand, building sand castles and burying each other. To me, the fairground was so exciting, the music, the fun rides made the day even more enjoyable. Even the journey to Barry and home again was a special experience. The crowds, the smells and the atmosphere were something that we did not experience very often, and we were always determined to enjoy these rare treats. Mam never had much in the way of money, but she always managed to pack enough food to keep us happy and we would save our pocket money for weeks to make sure we had enough to spend on ice cream and the fair.

If any of the children happened to get lost in the crowds, we would have to go to the lost children's compound, which was situated alongside the large amusement arcade, on the numerous times I got lost, I sat on a row of seats with other children until we were collected by our parents. I always seemed to spend quite some time sat in there, with people gazing at me as they walked by. Sometimes, it seemed I spent more time in there than on the beach.

The return journey home saw us all singing songs like 'I'll take you home again Kathleen', 'It's a long way to Tipperary', 'She'll be coming round the mountain' and many more. The three buses would stop on the way home at a fish and chip shop on the outskirts of Newport. We all queued along a long line of steps that led up to a house that had partly been converted into a fish and chips shop, and by the time everyone had managed to get served, we had spent about an hour there before returning home.

Pontypool in the 1940's

Early every summer, the Trinder boys told me how much they were looking forward to their summer holiday. Each year, they would travel to Hereford where they would go hop picking. I would be so jealous; I always wanted to go along with them. I did not really know what hop picking was or where Hereford was, but I knew it was something to do with putting hops into sacks to make beer.

A few days after we broke up school for the summer holidays, a large flatbed lorry with sides attached to it would come down Mill Road, turn around and stop outside the Trinders' house. Out came the whole family with the young ones carrying bags and the older members carrying luggage cases or boxes. They were all so excited and yelled to me that they were going to sleep in a barn full of hay for the next month and they wished that I could go with them.

The driver, Mr Trinder and Tommy would undo and drop down the sides of the lorry, lay out the blankets upon the floor and help the rest of the family to climb up. When everyone was seated, the cases and boxes would be loaded on and the sides would be lifted back up. After locking the front door, Mr Trinder would be the last to climb aboard and with a tap on the window, he would shout "Everything's alright, driver. We can go now!" and the lorry pulled away slowly up Mill Road.

I stood in the middle of the road and waved them goodbye. I felt sad and a little lonely and I wished I could have joined them. "Goodbye Brian, wish you could come with us. See you when we come home." I stood there until the lorry was out of sight. I missed them every time they left; summertime was so quiet without them.

Chapter 9

New arrivals

One evening in early 1949, just before bedtime, my mother sat beside me and explained that I was going to have a new baby brother or sister in May. I was so pleased and excitedly I asked her if I could have a brother so that I had someone to play with. I was keen for him to come and sleep in my bedroom and I asked if I could go along to the hospital to collect him. My only thoughts were that Mam took the baby to hospital in her tummy and then brought him home. I had no idea how it got there in the first place. John and Margaret told me that the baby got into Mam's tummy by her eating plenty of fresh warm bread from the bakery.

May arrived and as I left school on a warm sunny afternoon, I called into Aunty Marge's house with Michael and was informed that Dad had taken Mam into the Lydia Beynan Hospital in Newport, as it was time for the baby to arrive. I had to go to Grandad Jones's house to stay for a few weeks until they came home. Aunty gave me a small case of clean clothes that Mam had packed for me and we went to Cwmffrwdoer on Peake's bus to Grandad Jones's house.

Aunty Esme, Aunty Gwyn, Uncle Derek, and Uncle Billy were still living with Grandad and they made me feel so welcome. They really made a fuss of me and I loved staying with them at Pleasant View. Aunty Esme used to take me shopping with her to the local Co-op store nearby. I was fascinated by the counter assistant who would put the money and the bill into a small round container then screw it onto a holder above her head, pull a cord and the container would shoot across the shop on cables hanging above everyone's heads until it came to stop above the cashiers head. The cashier sat in a sort of cage in the corner of the shop with around five or so of these containers flying towards him. As they came to a stop, he would reach up, unscrew them and take out the money inside. He would read the amount on the bill for the goods and place the change back inside with the receipt. He would then pull another cord to return the container back to the counter assistant who would then give the change and receipt back to the customer.

Every day during my stay, I waited eagerly for Aunty Gwyn to return from work, as she always brought delicious cream cakes. I think she worked in a cake shop somewhere. I sat in the window at the front of the house and waited until she appeared coming up the road

There was a pathway at the back of Grandad Jones's house, which led to the house where Mam's oldest sister, Aunty Floss, lived with her husband Ivan Evans, her son Colin and daughters Audrey and Pearl.

I didn't really like walking into her back yard, as it was full of chickens which used to scare me. She always kept a big tin of sweets on her top shelf in her pantry, which she always filled my pockets with, so it was worth facing the chickens for this.

On the evening of May 16th 1949, Dad came bursting in through Grandad's front door and called my name excitedly. I ran over to him, he picked me up high into his arms as Grandad, Aunty Esme, and Aunty Gwyn looked on. "You have a baby brother," his said joyfully.

"What's his name, Dad?"

"It's Derek James George, after your Uncle Derek and each of your grandfathers."

"When can I see him?"

"In a few weeks, when we collect them from the nursing home."

"Does he look like me, Dad?"

"Not really, as he has jet black hair and brown eyes and you have fair hair and blue eyes."

"Oh never mind, I don't care as long as he can come and play with me!"

1953 Twmpath School class photo, I'm 3rd from right back row

Dad said that he wouldn't be able to play with me for a little while yet, as he was just a tiny baby. I couldn't wait to see him but dad said I had to stay with Grandad for a few weeks until he came for me in a car that he would borrow from his friend Alex Horton when he collected me, We sat in the car and waved goodbye to everyone and they shouted that we had to bring Mam and the new baby back to see them soon.

We travelled to the nursing home in Newport to collect them and returned home to Mill Road. I absolutely loved my new brother and was so proud to push him in his pram when we went shopping in Pontypool. Whenever I earned some money, I would go into the toyshop and buy him something to play with and when he took his first steps. I became even more excited at the thought that he would soon be able to play with me.

All this time, I was still working with my father with the grocery rounds every Saturday and during school holidays. We would get up early in the mornings and load the van and make deliveries until late in the evening.

In Twmpath School Uniform – I enjoyed my stay at Twmpath

Early in 1951, my mother told me that she was expecting another baby in the springtime and I was looking forward to having another little playmate. May came and Mam and Dad thought the baby would arrive on the same day as Derek's birthday, but the 16th came and went and there was still no baby. Two days later, Mam packed a little suitcase with clothes for Derek and me, but this time we went to Aunty Emily's house to stay with John and Margaret. Once again, my mother travelled to the Lydia Beynon hospital in Newport. Late the next day, Dad came up with the good news that we had a new baby sister. I was slightly subdued with this news, as I didn't think we would have a sister, only another brother.

"Oh well, I suppose it will be alright as she can play with Michael's baby sister Esme when she grows up. I suppose it's another cot in my bedroom?" I said to Dad, disappointingly.

"I'm afraid so, Brian. It's not your bedroom anyway; it is for the three of you. Don't you want to know her name?" Dad asked.

"Yes I suppose so;"

"It's Susan, Susan Marion."

"That's a nice name. Is she like Derek?"

"No she's like you, very fair."

"I guess she'll be alright then."

A few weeks later, Dad collected Mam and baby Susan from the nursing home in his van and then came for Derek and me. By then, I was very excited to see Mam and the new baby and wondered what she looked like. I walked into our house at Mill Road and there she was in her cot. As I gently pulled the clothes from over her face, she looked so little and so pretty. I asked if I could hold her and Mam said of course I could. She handed her to me and said to be careful as she was so tiny. I held her close to me and loved her from that moment onwards. There was a strong bond between us immediately. "I don't mind sharing my bedroom with you," I said, "You are most welcome."

The house seemed so full now with another child, but I loved them both very much, and still bought them toys with the little money that I had. I used to look after them for Mam to go shopping into town and then I would go to the cinema later.

Money became harder to get now with Dad working to keep the five of us. In June 1951, I was talking to David Phillips who lived three doors up from us. He worked for Bellamy's paper shop on the Clarence and he told me that there was an early morning paper round available. Miss Bellamy had asked him if he knew of anyone who was reliable who would like to take it on. He told me that I would have to arrive at the shop at 7.30am and put all the papers together from a list in the shop. I would have to write the correct house number on the top of the paper, place then in a canvas bag and deliver then to the houses in the Blaendare area. I could then either drop the bag back at the shop or take it home with me. David said that I would soon get used to it and to watch out for Fridays as the bag would be twice as heavy as everyone has the weekly local paper 'The Free Press'. I did not have to collect any money as everyone paid at the shop. I asked David how much I would be paid and he said five shillings a week, which I thought was quite good. I asked Mam and Dad if I could take the job and they said I could, as long as I got to school on time as the 11 plus test was coming up and they wanted me to pass so that I could go to West Mon Grammar school nearby.

The next day, I called into Bellamy's shop and as I entered the shop, the bell rang out and Miss Bellamy appeared. Her name was Marge and she was thin and tall with black hair and a long fringe above her eyebrows. Her lips were heavily covered in bright red lipstick. She was aged around 50 and all the paperboys used to call her lipstick face. She never married and lived above the shop with her elderly mother and she was always very firm when she spoke. She stood like a statue over me. "Can I help you?" she said.

"Dave Phillips spoke to me about the Blaendare round and I've come to ask you if I can have it please."

"You are Aubrey's boy, Brian aren't you?"

"Yes, Mrs Bellamy."

"It's Miss Bellamy please."

"Sorry."

"Yes, of course you can, if you are reliable that is. I know your Dad very well."

She took me into a small room at the back of the shop and explained how to put the papers together in order, from the stacks of papers that sat on various tables.

Miss Bellamy told me that I could start on the following Monday. I said that I would be there before eight and that she could rely on me without any worries at all.

Once my paper round duties began, I started saving my money every week. I dearly wanted to buy myself a second hand push bike and when I thought I had saved enough, I went down to the scrap dealers place down at Trosnant. I hoped Frank Harris had one suitable for me, but when I got there he said that he was sorry that he didn't have any, but he thought his brother Rag Harris might have one . I thanked him and made my way down, hoping all the way that he did have one. Rag wasn't his real name and I wondered why everyone called him by this strange name. I wasn't sure if any one at all knew what his real name was. I approached the scrap yard situated in the centre of it was a large neglected detached house that had seen better days.

"Hello Mr Harris," I said, as he emerged from in between a pile of scrap metal and the house itself. He was a large chubby man with a little black moustache and he was always wiping his hands with a dirty cloth. I thought he looked like the comedian Oliver Hardy and that everyone should have called him Ollie, not Rag.

"Hello son, haven't seen you here lately, no scrap then?" he asked.

"No, I started a paper round for Mrs Bellamy and with helping my Dad on his rounds, I've been pretty busy. Dad's not happy about me collecting any more since I cut my chin." He bent down and looked at my scar.

"Still a nasty mark there, lad so I don't blame him. What can I do for you then?"

"I've come to see if you have any bikes that might suit me Mr Harris."

"Well you've come to the right place." He walked over to an old shed at the end of the yard and pointed to two bikes. One was a little bigger than the other and he pulled out a black one, which looked a little worse for wear. It had two flat tyres and the chrome was tarnished, but it had a good small rack between the handlebars that was used to deliver goods at one time. "I want fifteen shillings for it," he said,

"It's not very good and needs a lot of work on it though," I replied with a glint in my eye hoping that I may get it a bit cheaper.

"I have a tin of black paint you can have and I will throw in some chrome cleaner."

I clutched the brake levers and offered him ten shillings explaining that I would have to buy a puncture kit to repair the tubes or buy some new tubes. Mr Harris agreed and the deal was done. "Make sure you do a good job then Brian," he said as he ruffled my hair.

I counted out the money from my little green money bag and Mr Harris then gave me a tin of black lacquer along with the chrome cleaner. I was very pleased as I went off pushing my bike up Trosnant Hill, being careful not to damage the flat tyres. The next Sunday, I spent all day striping it down, painting and repairing and putting coloured stickers on it. I was thrilled with the outcome, as it looked great. I treasured that old bike and used it to run errands for Mam, mainly up to Gregory's shop to pay her shoe bill and to collect groceries for some of the elderly people that lived up Mill Road.

I continued delivering papers six days a week for around three years and I never missed one morning. One advantage of the paper round was getting to know the news of the day. The war in Korea was continuing and the Festival of Britain was taking place in London. Everyone was hoping for a brighter future for Britain, now World War Two was over. The sad thing was that rationing was still taking place, but we hoped that this wouldn't be for too much longer.

Chapter 10

Failure and Success

June 1952 was now approaching and it was now time for me to sit the Eleven Plus examination for entry to a grammar or secondary modern school if you failed, I had been optimistic as I excelled at arithmetic and always came close to top of the class, especially with mental arithmetic. However, sadly came the result that I had failed. My English had obviously let me down and we were all so disappointed with the news.

I started at Twmpath Secondary Modern School on Monday 3rd of September 1952, aged twelve years and three weeks, with friends Glyn Horler, Kenny Blake, Tony Morgan and Billy Walker, as they had also failed the 11 plus exam.

I thoroughly enjoyed my time at Twmpath School. The relaxed and easy atmosphere was welcoming and Glyn and I became best friends. Glyn was an only child and seemed to have everything. Still he was a great friend to me. His father was one of the first to own a car in the area.I used to call into Billy Walker's house with my friend Michel Taylor and his brother Brian who lived a few doors away and we would sit on the floor and watch mainly cowboy films with Hopalong Cassidy and Roy Rogers on their small black and white television. The Walker's were the first family to have a set in Pontypool.

On the 29th of May 1953 news came that Mount Everest had been conquered, and a few days later on June the 2nd we saw the coronation of Queen Elizabeth on their set.

After almost a year attending Twmpath, the boys in my class had the chance to sit an exam for entry to a Technical school at Abersychan. Most of us took the exam and I really tried my best, but again, the result was disappointing. Billy had passed and Glyn and I had failed again. But by a twist of fate, a few days later we were both informed by post that we had been put on the reserve list.

It was an anxious few weeks before the postman delivered a letter informing me of the result. About a week before term began, I found Dad stood reading a letter from the school authorities. I took a deep breath and a cold shudder went through me, as I guessed what news it might contain. Dad glanced at me over his thick brown glasses, and then a smile came over his face as he told me the good news. I had been accepted for entrance to Abersychan Technical School.

Twmpath School sports day, June 1953 in Pontypool Park Stand

I was over the moon and Mam looked equally pleased. She said that we would have to go shopping for a new uniform. I would need a black jacket, gold tie and a school satchel. We went into the house and had some breakfast and I thought about Glyn and wondered if he had been accepted too. I asked Dad if I could go along to his house and see if he had received the news. Dad said that I should try not to appear too excited in case Glyn had not received the same result. The walk to Coe Cae where he lived it took me about fifteen minutes. I knocked on the door and his mother answered saying hello but looking a little surprised that I was so early. I said sorry but explained that I was eager to know if Glyn had passed his test to go to Abersychan Tec before I started with Dad on his round. "Come on in and ask him," she said and I walked in to find him eating his breakfast and reading his letter. "Well, have you passed?" I asked.

"Yes, I've been accepted," he said quietly, with a look of anticipation and hope that I had the same reply. "How about you Brian?"

"Yes Glyn I have, I got my letter this morning."

"What great news! We can go together on the bus from the Clarence bus stop."

"It's going to be great! Well, I have to go and help Dad on his rounds, so I'll see you soon. Goodbye Mrs Horler," I yelled, as I scurried out and headed home.

The next week Mam took me shopping for my school uniform in Pontypool town. We bought a black blazer, grey trousers and a gold and black tie. I also needed a satchel and Mam said that they sold them at Gregory's shoe shop on Hanbury Road that was a few hundred yards from Grandad's house at Cwmffrwdoer. We always bought our shoes there as Mam could pay for them on a weekly basis; instead of paying out for them all in one go, as we still had very little money. I rode my bike up to the shop every Monday and paid Mr Gregory a few shillings off her account. He would mark it down in the little pink book that I gave him which Mam always kept in her handbag at home. I looked forward to picking a new pair of shoes and a satchel and Mam proudly told Mr Gregory that I would be attending 'The Tec'. He said that he had a few satchels and reached up and pulled one off the shelf, saying that they were five shillings and very good value. My mother said that would be all right and asked for a new pair of black shoes for me. I held the satchel in my hand and thought it didn't look that good to me. It was brown and very thin leather and plastic buckles on the front, but I suppose it was all she could afford. We also bought a grey gabardine mackintosh for me to wear to school from the co-op in Pontypool.

On Monday the 1st of September 1953 I finished my paper round and rushed home to change into my new school uniform, eager to start my first day at the Technical school at Abersychan. It was a fifteen-minute bus ride from the Clarence bus stop up the valley towards Blaenavon. It was a rainy morning, I had arranged to meet Glyn at the bus stop at 8.30, and as I arrived, he was stood there waiting for me. He looked very smart in his expensive new grey gabardine mackintosh with padded shoulders and a neat waist belt. Over his shoulder hung his satchel that was a shiny bronze colour with metal buckles.

"Morning Glyn, are you alright?" I asked.

"Yes, and you Bri?"

"Ok, but a bit worried though. I hope I fit in alright up at this school."

"Of course you will. We can go into the same class together and I'll be with you so don't worry."

"That's a nice satchel you got, Glyn."

"Mam bought it me from Sharps the leather shop in town."

He glanced at my satchel and did not say anything, then looked down the road and spotted the bus approaching. The red and white Western Welsh school bus came alongside us and the conductor asked to see our free passes. We climbed aboard and took our seats. This took place every morning for the next two years. During my time at the school, I never really settled and wished that I could go back to Twmpath. The work was very difficult and many times, I cried to Dad pleading with him to send me back to Twmpath. All he ever said was that I should try it for a few more weeks. I suppose he was right, but it never really helped. When we finished school at 3.30, Glyn and I would be clutching our satchels that bulged with books and ran as fast as we could down the school lane. We were eager to be first in the queue to catch the bus home. I would sit in my bedroom every evening doing my homework, which I disliked very much.

A few months later, I had to go into Pontypool hospital to have my tonsils removed. It was winter and there was snow on the ground. The view from my window was the school route and I would watch the bus taking the children to school and think how lucky I was not to be on one of them.

One morning Mam asked me to go into Pontypool to buy some groceries and call into Moore's the butchers on the Clarence to collect a joint of meat and some black pudding before I started with Dad on his rounds. I decided to go on my bike, as I thought it would be quicker and when I arrived at the butchers, I stood my bike against the pavement with the stand. I went into the shop and stood in the queue against the counter at the rear of the shop until it was my turn. Mr Moore was a very tall and thin man with a baldhead. He wore thin reading glasses that rested on the end of his nose.

"Hello Brian, come for your mother's order have you?" he said, as he held his head down and peered over the top of his glasses.

"Yes please, Mr More."

"Aren't you on the rounds with your Dad today, Brian?"

"Yes, I'll catch up with him later when I've finished shopping for Mam."

"Alright, I'll hurry up then."

He went over to the shop window display and picked up a large joint of meat and at that moment, I heard a loud noise outside the shop. It was liked metal being crushed. Mr Moore leaned over, looked outside, and said he could see a lorry driver looking under his back wheel at something.

"I think it's a push bike or something"

I felt a cold shiver through my body, as I leaned against the counter, knowing that I had left my bike outside.

"Yes, I can see it now, it's a little black push bike and both the wheels are buckled. Anyone's in here?" he asked.

"I think it could be mine," I answered as I stepped forward towards the front door. I was trembling as Mr Moore opened it, hoping all the time that my bike was still intact. I came to a large green lorry and protruding out from behind the rear wheel was a mangled black frame with both the wheels twisted. I knew at once that it was mine, as I could see the stickers that I had stuck on the frame, raising from the damaged paint. I could not hold back the tears as I stood there looking down at my bike. I had spent so much time saving for it and doing it up and I was so upset to see it in the state it was. The lorry driver said he was sorry, but I was angry with him and asked him why he had done this as I wiped away the tears that ran down my face. The sleeve of my coat was wet from the salty tears and I just couldn't stop crying. I dragged the mangled frame from the road as the driver said that he couldn't help it. He said that he had tipped the handlebars over and it went underneath his back wheels. He spoke fretfully and Mr Moore said that I should go and get my dad quickly. It was clearly the driver's fault and Mr Moore assured me that he would not let him go until I had arrived back with Dad. Dad had not left for his rounds and he came straight back up with me. The driver asked Dad not to report him, as he was concerned that he may lose his job. He asked for our address and said that he would definitely get me another bike and bring it up from Cardiff for me. Dad, being as trusting as he was, agreed not to report him but did not ask for his name and address and I waited for weeks for the driver to come back but he never did. Sadly, I was the one that lost out. I began saving my paper round money again and bought another bike a few months later from the scrap yard. I did not really learn my lesson though as I still trusted people, but I remained upset that someone could be so deceitful to me.

On my way home from school one day during the winter of 1953, I came to Aunty Marge's house and noticed that Mam was outside on the door step waving for me to come in. "Brian, come on inside, Aunty Marge has something to tell you." I stepped inside the house that I knew so well, and there sat Aunty with Jean and Michael, along with Esme and Mary, and they all looked very excited.

"Brian, I have something to tell you. Uncle George has a new job in the coalmines in Staffordshire and we'll be moving to a new Cornish style house in Stoke-on-Trent. It'll be a new beginning for us."

I could not believe it and felt very much alone knowing that Aunty would not be living near to me. I could not imagine not being able to see Michael each day and I felt that I was doomed to stay at Mill Road.

"Will you be gone forever Aunty? Won't I see you again?" I asked as my eyes filled with tears. She put her arms around me and held me close. "Of course you'll be able to see us. You can come and visit any time." Michael stood up and came towards me.

"Don't upset yourself, we'll have some good times together I'm sure, when you come up to visit us, and don't forget, I'll be back to see you."

"When are you going, Aunty?" I said, as I wiped away my tears.

"In about two week's time. We're arranging a school for Jean and Michael, and then we have to pack all our things and empty the house." Esme and Mary were too young to understand the enormity of the situation, and they just sat listening.

Pontypool in the 1950s

The following few weeks went by very quickly. My mother spent some time helping Aunty Marge pack and I spent some time with Michael and Tony Gust, as Tony and I knew we would not be seeing him for a long time. The day arrived for them to depart. They were travelling by train from Pontypool Road Station, New Inn, to Stoke. A lorry had loaded their belongings and gone ahead to Stoke that morning. Mam and I went with them on the bus to the station and when we arrived, the platforms were very busy. We stood there with all the Smith family and we felt a little sad, but they were tinged with the excitement of going to a new house and a different place to live.

The huge steam train slowly pulled into the station and came to a stop at the end of the platform. We all hugged each other closely and I secretly hoped that they would turn around and change their minds about leaving. As they entered the carriage, I shouted "Goodbye and see you all again one day." The train then pulled away slowly with them all inside waving frantically. How lonely I felt inside as I stood on the same platform that I used to leave from to travel to Halifax during the war…

"Goodbye Aunty Marge," I shouted, as I waved a final time to the carriage that was disappearing into a cloud of steam in the distance. It felt so different passing Auntie's house every day from then on. It stood empty until the day it was pulled down with some other houses around it, a few years later.

Chapter 11

Any cake scrapes please?

I continued helping my father every Saturday on his grocery round and spending most evenings after school doing my homework and visiting the cinemas with John Jenkins, Norman's oldest son and Cousin John Rowland. We saw films that starred Dean Martin and Jerry Lewis along with Norman Wisdom, but my screen idol was Tony Curtis. I continued saving my paper round money and soon had enough to purchase a Parlaphone 'wind up' gramophone player that played 78 inch records. It had a handle on the side that played two records for every 'wind up'. I was thrilled to bits with it and the first record I bought was 'I'll be Home' by Pat Boone. Johnny Ray was my favourite at the time. I used to travel on the bus to Cardiff to a shop called Spillers Records on the Hayes, to buy his records. I also kept a scrapbook of any news and photos that I came across.

Sadly, around this time, my brother Derek had caught polio and he spent about nine months in a hospital near Chepstow. I went to visit him every Sunday for several years, his one leg had to be kept in a metal brace that the doctors called 'irons'. This was because one leg was growing quicker than the other was. He eventually recovered much to the relief of us all and he grew into a good-looking boy with very dark hair. His colouring was very different to Susan's and mine as we were very fair.

Towards the end of the summer soon after my 13th birthday, Cousin John Rowland and I were now firm friends. We went everywhere together and I often spent the night at his house. John had an evening job serving petrol from the pumps at Norman Jenkins' petrol station near the Clarence. He asked how many gallons the customers required and put the petrol into their tank. Sometimes I would sit in the office with him and we would chat in between him serving customers.

One evening as I sat there with John, Mr Barrell the man who was the owner of The Carlton Bakery, called in one of his vans for some petrol. I knew him quite well as his drivers delivered bread down Mill Road and called to our house. He was a nice quiet man and looked just as you would imagine a typical baker should look. He had a chubby round face with glowing pink cheeks. He was married, but did not have any children and he was about fifty years old. The bakery was situated around two hundred yards away behind the Clarence Hotel. The three of us began talking and John said how lucky he was to have an evening job, as the money he earned came in useful as it enabled him to go to different places. Mr Barrell then informed us that he was looking for a lad to work in the evenings after school to slice and wrap bread and load it onto the vans ready for the next morning. He also needed someone to help at busy holiday times. He asked if I would be interested, as he knew that I was reliable as I delivered his papers to his home on time and without fail. I thought about it for a moment and remembered my early morning paper round and how I got up so early and sometimes came home cold and wet before going to school. I thought that maybe I could give up my paper round as I had been doing it for a few years, and the thought of working in a warm bakery and probably getting more money gave me a cosy feeling inside. I told Mr Barrell that I would like to work for him, but I would have to ask Mam and Dad if it was all right with them.

"Can I call in tomorrow around 5 o'clock in the evening and let you know?"

"Of course you can Brian, see you tomorrow then," he answered as he got into his van and drove away.

John and I started chatting and thought how great it would be if I were able to take the job. We could still go to the pictures after we finished work and we could afford to go to Cardiff and see the shows. I agreed and then rushed home as I had homework to do.

Later that evening, I told Mam and Dad the news and Dad said it would be fine to take the job, providing that I did my homework. He advised me to keep my paper round going for a while until I was sure that things worked out ok. I agreed and looked forward to telling Mr Barrell. Dad asked if I could still help him out on his rounds on a Saturday and I said of course and that I would do my homework on a Sunday.

That evening, when Susan and Derek had gone to bed (I always waited for them to go to sleep first), I led in bed thinking about my new job and how nice it would be to work in the warm atmosphere of the bakery and with the lovely smell of freshly baked bread.

The next day I told my mother that I would be going up to the bakery after school to have a chat with Mr Barrell. I said I would probably be a while, as Mr Barrell would be showing me around and letting me know what

I would be doing. When I had finished school, I walked up to the bakery along a footpath that ran alongside the tip. As I stood and faced the front of the building to the right side was a small covered yard where two delivery vans were parked. To the left of the yard at the side of the bakery, there was a wooden door, the entrance to the bakery. On each side, of the door there were six wooden shelves where the bread was stacked, after it came out of the ovens to cool down.

I knocked on the door and a voice answered saying "just a minute". The door opened and Mr Barrell stood there with his white apron on. His hair covered in flour and his pink cheeks were a prominent feature on his face.

"Hello Brian, come on in," he said, as he walked back to a table that had trays full of cakes on it. He was covering the tops of the cakes with pink icing. They looked delicious and I was immediately hit with the appetising smell of fresh cakes and bread. I knew I was going to enjoy it here and Mr Barrel made me feel very welcome. He looked across at me, as I stood staring at the surroundings; there were wooden tables everywhere with strange machines between them. To the right of me stood two large black iron doors, one above the other, with a large lever attached to them. These were the doors to the ovens.   "I'm glad you came," he said, wiping is hands in his apron. "I expect it's about the job so I'd better tell you about the money first. Its ten shillings a week for slicing the bread, which takes about an hour and a half each evening. I will give you more if I need you to help me in the bakery to get the cakes ready for the morning. We get very busy around bank holiday times and at Christmas, so I'll give you more money at these times. Is that alright with you, Brian?" he asked.

"Yes of course. I am happy to help and Mam and Dad said it would be good to work for you, Mr Barrell."

"Good. I'll show you around and you can start tomorrow evening if you like."

I agreed and Mr Barrell began to show me the system. He said that they began about 5 o'clock in the morning, making the bread and that he had two men working for him, brothers Peter and Ken Mahoney. They made the dough in one of the machines that stood in the corner of the bakery. It looked like a huge bowl that was around four feet high and ten feet in diameter and had a huge lid. Inside was a large winged shaft that spun around. He pointed to a large stack of one hundred weight sacks of flour and said that they put three sacks of flour into the 'bowl' and then add several packs of yeast to make the dough rise. He showed me some of the yeast and I thought it looked like glass putty. Then they added water from a glass tank, which was on brackets on the wall above the 'bowl'. There was a pipe coming from the tank and a tap that let in the required amount of water. The lid would then be closed and the machine switched on Ten minutes later, the dough would be ready.

The next step was to feed the dough into a different machine, which looked very complex. It stood by the only window in the room, and you could see out over Mill Road from it, when the machine was switched on the dough was piled into the hopper and measured each piece of dough into the right size and it came out the other end on to a belt. The pieces would then be put into metal baking tins, which were usually in a row of fours, each one the size of a loaf of bread. He explained that this occurred until all the dough had been used up, and then would then be left for an hour until the dough had risen. All the tins were then placed into both of the ovens with twelve foot wooden poles. The end of the poles was wide and flat and they were kept alongside the ovens.

Mr Barrell showed me how to open the oven doors with the long handle and as he did, a blast of hot air came out instantly. I was a little startled at the fierce heat and I began to perspire immediately. I sheltered my face and Mr Barrell said that I would soon get used to it. He then put the four tins onto the flat end of the pole and slid them down to the rear of the ovens until both ovens were full. He called this a batch, which he explained was about six hundred loaves. Half an hour later, the bread was baked. He then slid the tins back out of the oven and onto a metal table, which was positioned close to the oven door. Peter or Ken would pick them up with their gloves on and place the four loaves onto the table. The other would carry the loaves into the yard and put them onto the shelves to cool. This process had to be carried out quickly as the bread at the rear could get burnt. Mr Barrell and I proceeded to the yard and the drop in temperature was most welcome. "I'm not keeping you, am I, Brian?"

"No Mr Barrell, I'm glad you're showing me. I'm very interested in how it all works."

He then went on to tell me that around 8 o'clock, both van drivers arrived to load their vans with the bread and cakes. Len drove the big van until around 3 o'clock and delivered to the houses. Gwen drove the small van and delivered to the shops and she usually finished around 12 o'clock. All the cakes were baked in the evening and were ready to go out with the bread the next morning. The sliced bread was the leftovers from the previous day as they were too hot to slice in the morning.

The sliced bread was packed during the evening and then loaded into the van in readiness for the next morning deliveries. Mr Barrell explained that this would be my job. I was also expected to help him in the bakery if there weren't many loaves to cut. We went through to the back of the bakery, passed the ovens on our way to the bread slicing machine. The heat was intense and I wondered how I was going to work in such hot conditions. I was determined to do a good job and remained positive regardless of the heat. The ovens were fed by a huge stack of coal which was kept at the rear of the yard.

"we've got a small separate warehouse at the back of the building, where I store all the things needed like the icing sugar, colouring essence, icing bags, large tins of fruit currants and sultanas. I also keep the bread cutting machine there. We haven't had it that long but it seems to be the bread of the future with more and more people asking for sliced bread." He opened a large door at the rear of the yard and switched on the light and proudly showed me the machine. It looked menacing with its sharp silver blades and large lever at the side. It reminded me of the way a hangman would use his trapdoor on the gallows. There were a few uncut loaves to the side of the machine and Mr Barrell gave me a quick demonstration. The whole of the machine began to vibrate and the blades shook up and down wildly. He began to speak loudly as there was quite a noise. "Pull the lever towards you and you'll see the previous loaf emerge from the blades. When it's clear, get an elastic band from the box on the side and stretch it around the bread to keep it together and stack it on the table next to the wrapping machine." He picked up another few loaves and carried out the same task until there were several on the table. "There, now you try it."

I picked up a loaf and slid it to the back of the machine and then slowly pulled the lever until the previous loaf appeared. I put a band around it and placed it onto the table and I repeated the same exercise a few times, growing a little more confident each time. Mr Barrell then ask me to wrap them and he sighed as if to warn me that this may be more difficult. The wrapping paper had the words 'The Carlton Bakery' printed on it. I had to pick up a loaf and place it on the centre of the paper. Mr Barrell explained that the paper had wax on it and I had to pull each end over each other and then wrap both ends together. He then showed me a small machine with two heated guides and he pushed the wrapped loaf through the guides where the heat melted the wax within the paper. As it cooled, the wrapping was completed. "Now you try, Brian."

The first few times, I ruined some sheets, but after a few attempts, I began to do a very good and quick job. Mr Barrell then showed me where to stack the bread on the vans, ready for the morning. I offered to do all the loaves that were left in the warehouse to make sure that I could do them on my own and he thanked me as he was very busy. I finished slicing and wrapping, all the time being careful to do a good job. Once I had finished, I made sure that I switched everything off and then loaded up the vans. I really wanted to do a good job and hoped Mr Barrell would be impressed with my willingness to help. I called to him that I had finished and he thanked me, saying he would see me tomorrow evening. He said that if he wasn't there, I was to go on up to the warehouse and begin my work.

"Thanks, Mr Barrell. I think I'm going to like working for you. See you tomorrow!" I went home happily looking forward to my new evening job and I couldn't wait to tell Mam, Dad, Susan and Derek all about what I had learnt.

The next day, I called in to see John to tell him that I was going to start work at the bakery, he was really pleased. He said that he would be over later to see how I was progressing. When I arrived at the bakery, there was no-one around. I though Mr Barrell had gone home for his evening break as he did every day. On some occasions, his wife would come back with him to help out with the cakes. I went into the warehouse and began my tasks and soon enough, Mr Barrell came in and asked me how I was getting on. I told him that I was doing fine and was about half way through completing and he said that he didn't need me for anything else that evening. I loaded the vans and went to say goodbye. Mrs Barrell came over to say how pleased she was to hear that I was working for them. I noticed that the couple never seemed to go anywhere, especially Mr Barrell who worked from early in the morning to late at night every day, apart from a Sunday when he and his wife went driving in the countryside of Chepstow and Monmouth. His car was a magnificent dark green Armstrong Sidley sapphire saloon with cream leather seats. Sitting proudly on the front of the bonnet sat an emblem of the car maker which was a small chrome statue of an Egyptian Sphinx. He was very proud of his car, but not in a pompous way as he worked hard and deserved to have some luxuries. I was lucky enough to travel in it on a few occasions and I specifically enjoyed going to see the Bertram Mills Circus at Monmouth. I felt so pleased as I sat there in this beautiful car and they treated me just like a son. Sometimes, I helped out in the bakery and I had to wear a white t-shirt and apron as I helped with the cakes. I was fascinated by it all and loved helping with the decorating of the cakes. I used to place the jam into the jam tarts and insert the cream into the doughnuts. I also sliced through the large round sponge cakes, spread jam and cream inside them and packed them into cellophane bags.

The job that I liked best was spreading the icing over the large trays of ice custard slices and cutting them into squares. I also cut the spare ends off them around the tray. Times were still hard and rationing was still taking place and most evenings there was a knock at the door and Mr Barrell would ask me to go and answer it. Mostly it was one of the poor young boys from either Trosnant or Mill Road asking for some scrap ends of cakes. Sometimes it was Terry or Dennis Trinder, but mostly it was Michael Trinder who was then only about eight years old.

"Any scraps left over please?" he would ask as he looked up at me, cold and with a runny nose, his hands stuck in the pockets of his grey scruffy coat to keep them warm.

"I'll ask Mr Barrell now," I would reply.

"Any scrap ends available, Mr B?"

The answer was always the same. "Make up a bag for them Brian, you know what's left over." He would never refuse any of them.

I opened the door a little wider and pointed at the floor and told them to stand in a certain spot. Whoever it was would stand just inside while I closed the door, I always felt good that I was in a position to help them.

I would go to the cupboard and get out a large paper bag and walk around the bakery filling it with crooked jam and custard tarts, and the waste edges of iced slices.

I'd previously cut the large trays of iced slices into squares, the edges were not used, so I always cut them wide for there to be plenty left over for the scraps to give to the boys, knowing that there would be a knock at the door later on. Sometimes, we gave them loaves that were undersized, but I suspected that they enjoyed the cakes the most. I felt so fortunate as I handed over the bag of cake ends and let them out through the door with a wink and a nod. All the boys in the area were so pleased when I opened the door as they knew they were in for some treats.

Chapter 12

School Ends

1954, and I considered my evening job at the bakery secure and I decided to give up my paper round as the early mornings and late evenings made my days seem long. With my homework and helping Dad with his round, it was becoming hard work. Dad began selling ice cream from two large tubs that he bought from an Italian family called Jake Savinie, who had an ice cream factory and a café in Pontypool town. There were a few Italian families living in the area, including Aldo Bragasie and Gus Pelopieda who had cafes on the Clarence and Savinies, Sidolies and Mario's who also had businesses in Pontypool town centre The Italians with their cafes and restaurants were very popular and well liked in the Welsh valleys.

I had been saving the money I earned from my paper round, and my job at the bakery, and thought that I had enough money to buy a new bike. John and I went into town together as he was also looking to buy one. We asked our parents if it was ok to go ahead and they agreed saying that it was our money and we could spend it if we liked as we had worked hard for it. It was a fantastic feeling and I felt so proud and lucky that I had accomplished my aim. I was having a new bike after years of old, used ones. I used to look on with envy at the boys who lived on the 'upper side' or 'above the Clarence' who always rode around on new bikes. Trosnant and Mill Road were always referred to as 'below the Clarence', but I never felt any resentment about this.

John and I went along to Saunders Bike shop in town, knowing that they always had a good selection of bikes in stock. We knew we could afford one as we looked in through the large window. We stared at the gleaming bikes and among them were two 'BSA' dropped handle bar racing bikes. One was red and the other was green and they were both the right size for us. The price tag on both was 3 pounds and 10 shillings. We knew at once that these were the bikes for us and John said he liked the green one and I was happy with the red. We went inside and behind the counter stood Mr Saunders. He was a small tiny man with grey sparse hair. He was short sighted and wore a pair of enormous thick glass spectacles. His eyes looked like two tiny dots behind them, but he needed them to read and count his money. He would hold up the notes very close to his eyes and he always seemed a miserable old grump.

"Hello, is there anything you want?" He said with a tone that meant that we had better not be wasting his time.

"Yes please Mr Saunders. We would like to have a look at the two 'BSA's' in the shop window. They are 3 pounds and 10 shillings each."

He peered at us from beyond his specs and said "I'm not getting them out unless you're serious about them."

"Yes Mr Saunders, look we've got the money but we want to make sure they are suitable for us."

His sallow face began to beam and his mouth widened slowly.

"Alright then, I'll pass them out to you."

He slowly eased past the other bikes and passed out the two we had requested to see.

"I'll adjust everything for you now." He said as he pulled out a spanner from behind the counter. We both sat astride the bikes trying out the brakes and simulating cycling along the road, while Mr Saunders made the necessary adjustments to the handle bars and saddles.

"There you go boys, I think they're alright now don't you?"

"Yes, they're great. Can we take them home with us today sir, if we pay now?"

"Of course you can. I'll get my receipt book." He said with eagerness in his voice. We paid for our bikes and walked through town and headed to the park. No traffic was allowed here and we knew it was a safe place to practise riding and working the gears. We had never had gears before but we soon got used to them. We cycled to both our parents' homes to show them and they were so pleased for us. John and I had good times together riding our bikes and going to Usk and Abergavenny at weekend. I was still busy helping Dad with his rounds every Saturday and we were still living at Mill Road.

An event that made the history books this year was that on 6th of May, Roger Bannister had broken the four minute mile. It was a milestone for British athletics. A few weeks after this news, the government announced the lifting of foodstuffs like meat and housewives the length and breadth of the country rejoiced.

I continued to attend Abersychan Technical School and still disliked my lessons very much. It seemed as though the teachers were not very dedicated to our education and spent their days reciting from books, informing us about the rock formation of the Andes, along with many other tedious topics that seemed to have no relevance to my future. One of the teachers was called Saunty Smith and all he ever did was pick his nose the flick it around the classroom! I suppose I would have taken more notice if I hadn't worked in the bakery. My heart was there and I enjoyed my work immensely, especially during the cold winter months when it was so warm and cosy inside. I never really wanted to go home to bed as it was so cold with the draughty windows and bitterly chilly bedroom. The view from my window grew worse as the refuse tip got closer and closer as time went by.

Reese was always repairing Dad's van, and always moaned that it was his fault when things went wrong blaming his poor driving technique. I often went to his garage on a Sunday morning and watched him repair cars and many times I thought that if I didn't have my job in the bakery then I would like to become a mechanic. I liked to help Uncle Rees with his invoices as I know he had difficulty with writing and I often went to the post office for him. "Thanks Bottle," he would say. I still wondered why he called me that name.

As Christmas approached, I saved my money hard and looked forward to a shopping trip into Pontypool to buy presents for Mam, Dad, Derek and Susan. I would take the presents to the warehouse at the back of the bakery and pack them neatly in Christmas paper and hide them there until Christmas Eve. I took great pleasure in giving them all their presents on Christmas morning and loved to see the surprise on Derek and Susan's faces as they lit up the room in excitement.

March 1955, I came home from school and found Mam very upset. She had received news from her brother, Uncle Billy that Grandad Jones had passed away. We were all very sad as he was a grand old man who I had fond memories of as a young lad. Mam and Dad went up to Grandad's house with Uncle Billy and I stayed at home to look after Derek and Susan. He was laid to rest the following week at Trevethin cemetery in the same grave as my grandmother Carrie.

The other news around this time was that Sir Winston Churchill had resigned from office and the conservatives won the general election with Sir Anthony Eden becoming our new Prime Minister.

A few days latter came the tragic news that a motor car had lost control in the Le Mans 24 hour race in France and ploughed into the crowd killing 77 spectators. This prompted a tightening of security among the racing authorities and major changes in track safety. John and I enjoyed motor racing very much and Sterling Moss was our hero. He went on to win the British Grand Prix that July at Aintree.

July 1955 saw Ruth Ellis hung at Pentonville Prison after being found guilty of murdering her lover, the racing driver David Blakely. The case increased tensions among many and there was much debate about our criminal justice system and the death penalty. The outcome was that she was the last woman to be hung in Britain.

It was a lovely warm and summer and as August approached, so did the end of my school days. I decided that engineering or building wasn't for me. I was very happy working at the bakery but I did know that I would have to look for some other work, as Mr Barrell already employed two men on a full time basis and didn't need any additional full time help. I was looking forward to finishing school, but had no idea what I would be doing when I left. Dad was eager for me to think about what I wanted to do and suggested that I work as an apprentice at a local factory or maybe work on the railways. I had no idea what they did in factories or what work they did on the railways. I only knew what an engine driver did and thought to myself that only old men were engine drivers.

One evening late in June came a turning point that decided my immediate future. As I carried out my tasks at the bakery, Mr Barrell called to me explaining that he had something important to discuss with me. He asked me to make a cup of tea and spoke with an unfamiliar but still friendly tone. We sat next to the small table that was kept in the corner of the bakery. We always sat here to have a cup of tea and I felt a little nervous as to what he was about to say. I worried that I had done something wrong or even worse, I feared that he was going to let me go as he knew I was about to leave school and would be classed as an adult. After all, it was only a part time, cash in hand job. He sat next to me and said "Well Brian, I have some news that I think may interest you, but don't tell anyone else yet please. Ken and Peter have given me their notice and will be finishing in two weeks time at the beginning of July. Gwen, who you know is one of our van drivers, her husband Graham Williams will be starting to work here full time when they leave." He leaned back in his chair in anticipation of my reaction. "Well, that's a surprise Mr Barrell. I thought Ken and Pete would be here forever. I know Graham, he's a great guy. He drives a milk van around the roads."

"Yes, he's a decent man; Ken and Pete are going into that new British Nylon Factory."

I sat and thought for a few seconds and realised that surely Mr Barrell would need another full time worker and I went ahead and asked if he had anyone else in mind. It was then that Mr Barrell asked if I would like to work for him full time, when my school days ended   He said that he was sure I would do a good job as he was very pleased with the job I was doing for him. He said that it would mean very early mornings. I was dumbfounded as it had never occurred to me that this opportunity would arise as I thought Ken and Pete were so settled and would be there for years to come.

"I don't know what to say, I never gave it a thought. But yes of course, I would love to come and work for you full time Mr Barrell. This is such a surprise though!"

"It's surprised me too son, I thought the lads were happy here but I guess it's just a job and the future prospects of working for a small firm like this, compared to a big factory may not be that appealing. I will have to speak to your father and get his opinion that is if you're really sure about working here full time?"

"I would love to Mr Barrell. I will tell Dad the news tonight and ask him to come and see you tomorrow evening."

Mr Barrell and I spoke at length about the forthcoming prospect and what Graham and I would do as part of our new roles. I felt a little apprehensive as he was around ten years older than me, but I was sure that things would work out fine.

When I spoke to Dad about the job offer, he said that he didn't mind me working at the bakery, but he was disappointed that I hadn't studied harder at school and had not gained some qualifications. He had hoped that I would become an apprentice in one of the factories and wished that I had paid a little more attention in my lessons. I felt slightly disappointed that maybe I had let Dad down and thought that I should have perhaps got some qualifications as they were required if you wanted a job in most factories. I also thought that I had been helping Dad on his rounds every weekend for the past seven years and I had also had my paper round and been working in the bakery. I had been so busy, I had very little time left for school and study and I had not been thinking about my future. Sometimes I had felt envious of the boys who were free to go playing football or swimming in the summer while I went to work with my father especially in the winter when it was bitterly cold. But not once did I regret helping my father as I loved him very much and it was a privilege to be of help to him.

Dad went to see Mr Barrell and they agreed that I could begin work in a week or so after school had finished.

On Friday 16th of July, I said farewell to my school days and told my friends where I would be working. I'm sure they thought that this really wasn't such a good job, but I knew that I would be happy there and with no qualifications, maybe this was my only choice.

The following Monday, I awoke very early and quietly left the house. I began work at 6am at the Carlton Bakery along with Mr Barrell and Graham. I thought Graham was very smart and he reminded me of Paul Newman. He was a ladies man and had a talent for singing.

I would love to hear him impersonate Frank Sinatra and Billy Daniels. He had started work a few weeks before me so he knew what he was doing. He was always very kind to me and we got on very well.

The first job of the day was baking the bread. Around one thousand loaves in two batches took around five hours to make. After making the dough in the huge mixing bowl, we gathered it with sharp knives and fed it into the hopper of the weighing machine that measured and cut the dough. It then came out the other end with each piece weighing approximately two pounds. We then put each piece into a row of four tins which later went into the ovens when the dough had risen.

Around five hundred loaves were placed into two ovens for forty five minutes until they were baked. The loaves were emptied onto a metal table and carried out onto racks in the yard to cool. This work was done in very hot conditions and we had to be quick. We then loaded the loaves onto the delivery vans, ready for when the drivers arrived to deliver them.

When the bread was completed, several large mixing bowls of pastry were made and cooked and used for iced slices and various assortments of tarts and sponge cakes. We usually finished work at about 3 o'clock in the afternoon, however Mr Barrell

Worked in the evenings completing the cakes and some evenings I went up to help him. I continued to answer the door and gave scrap cake ends to all my friends who knocked on the bakery door.

Chapter 13

The Rock and Roll Years

My fifteenth birthday arrived on the 6th of August and it was a sunny Saturday. Mam had arranged a small party outside our house for the evening and John Rowland and all the boys from the street came along. I wished that Aunty Marge would turn up as I missed her so much, but she was unable to travel back. I understood as I knew that Stoke on Trent was a long way away.

To my surprise, Mr Barrell and Graham called in and they presented me with a specially made large round birthday cake. I was touched that they thought so much of me to go to the trouble of arranging this treat. Even Mam and Dad seemed happier these days which in turn made me happy.

On the 30th of September 1955, I sat listening to Variety Band Box on the radio and I heard the sad news that the American film star James Dean had been killed in a tragic road accident while driving his sports car. This was a few days after he had finished filming "Giant "which he starred in, with Elizabeth Taylor. He was just twenty four years old and was destined to have a glittering Hollywood career.

In November 1955, a new face appeared at Norman's garage to train as a mechanic. It was Michael Taylor, who lived near to Billy Walker, house, who we used to watch television with after we left school. Mike was a dark curly haired, good-looking boy who reminded me of my screen idol, Tony Curtis.

It was still a time when children were very much expected to be seen and not heard but teenagers were finding a voice of their own and like James Dean, they were beginning to express themselves loudly and rebelliously. It was a catalyst that youth culture required to make an anti adult and anti authority stance.

Rock Around The Clock by Bill Haley and his Comets was a recording first heard in the opening titles of the film 'The Blackboard Jungle' that came to the Cinemas towards the end of 1955 and topped the charts for five months. In the Months that followed the film Rock Around The Clock was released and along with this song and a few other rock and roll songs it caused disturbances at some cinemas. This behaviour worried many adults who regarded the music as debased and deeply troubling. John and I went with some of our mates to see the film at the Capitol Theatre in Newport, but we certainly didn't see any trouble and we hadn't heard of any problems in South Wales.

As we entered 1956, I had been working full time at the bakery for four months. The request for fresh 'sliced wrapped' bread was increasing dramatically. Some of the shops that we supplied bread to were complaining to the van drivers that we were not fulfilling their requirements as we were not able to supply fresh sliced bread daily each morning.

This was becoming a real concern and we all worried that the loss in trade was beginning to affect us. As I pondered the position, I wondered what I could do to help the situation. I worked out a plan in my head and quietly suggested it to Mr Barrell and Graham. I thought that the only way that we could supply our customers with fresh sliced bread was by working nights.

As I put my idea forward, there was a silent reaction from them. I worried that they may have thought that I was too young to come up with such an idea or that it was ok for me to come up with the suggestion as I didn't really have home and family life pressures like they did being a young single lad. It didn't matter to me if I worked days or nights and I knew that Mam and Dad didn't mind either.

"I guess you don't mind working nights, son if you have to?" Mr Barrell enquired with a look of relief on his face.

"I don't really want to, but I would if you asked me to."

Graham didn't say anything at first, he just listened. I knew he wasn't keen on the idea. After a few minutes, he asked how my idea would work and I explained that I would begin work at 10 o'clock each evening and start mixing the dough. Mr Barrell and Graham would come in at 11 o'clock and we could all start feeding the hopper and completing the first batch of bread which would be out of the oven and on the racks by 2 o'clock. It would be ready for slicing no later than 4 o'clock. I could then take the loaves to the warehouse and slice and wrap them ready for the van drivers and while I did this, Mr Barrell and Graham could prepare the second batch of bread. I figured that this was the only way we could supply as much sliced bread as was required. I explained my plan as I sat on the table and I felt like a young school boy with Mr Barrell and Graham casting their eyes over me. I had the feeling that Graham didn't like the idea at all.

I walked over to the area where the tea was made. I winked across the room at Mr Barrell and said "Think about it while I make the tea." I must have sounded very sure of myself and even a little cocky. As I made the tea, things remained quiet, but just then I heard Mr Barrell say that he supposed that I was right and he had thought about it when Ken and Pete worked for him but he knew they would never go for it, so he had never mentioned it.

We were all aware that demand for the product was increasing and this was the only way that our customers would remain happy. We knew that if we did not change our working ways, they would go elsewhere and the business would be unable to operate. Graham reluctantly agreed and we had an open and honest conversation. Both agreed that they would speak to their wives first and the following morning, we agreed to begin our new working patterns from the following Sunday. From then on, we worked six nights a week and had every Saturday night off. The strategy was a success and Mr Barrell had to increase the amount of bread from two batches a night to three to achieve the extra demand for sliced bread. With the extra work and revenue, we received a substantial increase in our wages.

I opened my first Bank account at Lloyds Bank in Pontypool, on January 1956 and I gave Mam and Dad extra money each week besides 'my keep' to enable them to rent a black and white 16 inch television from Redifusion. It was such a thrill to have our own set and so much better than having to visit someone else's home to watch theirs.

There were some sad memories in the bakery as well as good. Mrs Barrell always kept two cats on the premises. She loved animals and always brought their food in for them. They were really there to catch any mice or rats that were tempted to enter the grounds to scavenge for food. One was called Sooty and the other called Misty.

Once a month, the ovens were shut down on a Saturday morning to enable the ashes to be cleared and the clinkers to be removed. They were then re-lit on Sunday evening. This job was always done by Mr Barrell. One Sunday evening, I started work about half past ten and was aware of a strange unusual smell in the air. The first job was always to put down the cat's milk dishes but I noticed that only Sooty came to drink it.

I carried on mixing the dough in the big mixer when Mr Barrell arrived.

"Everything alright, Brian?" he said, cheerfully.

"Yes, Mr B, but I can smell something different somewhere."

"I expect it's a loaf left in the oven from last week. It's probably black by now."

"No, I don't think so, it seems like some meat to me."

Just then, Graham arrived and said "What's that smell?"

"We don't know," Mr B answered.

I then began to think about the cats and said "I don't want to alarm you, Mr B, but I haven't seen Misty yet. She never came for her milk."

A shocked look came over his face and he turned white and walked over to the closed oven doors. He pulled the big lever of the bottom oven as a gush of hot air came out with a strong smell of burnt hair and meat. "Oh no!" he shouted out as he peered inside the oven. "I think it must be Misty."

The three of us were shocked and upset. Mr B held back his feelings and looked helpless, his voice sounded very dismayed as he said "It's my fault. When I came in and lit the ovens this evening, I shut both doors to keep the heat in, unknown to me, she must have crept in there this morning. I never thought they would ever go in there."

"It's not your fault, you didn't know she was in there," Graham said sympathetically.

"I don't know what my wife will say, She'll be ever so upset". .

I felt dreadful for him and said "Listen Mr B, there's no need for her to know what's happened. We can just say I found her curled up in between two sacks of flour." Graham agreed. "That's what we'll say, if you like Mr Barrell?"

"Thanks chaps, I don't like telling lies, but she'll feel terrible about what happened and there's no reason for her to know really."

Graham went to the back of the ovens and brought with him the long rake that was used to clean the ashes out.

"Go and make us some tea, Mr B," Brian and I will sort Misty out"

"Get an old flour sack, Brian while I get her out of here" he said as He scraped the charred remains towards the oven door, then into the sack we then went out and buried her in an area of green grass at the rear of the Clarence Hotel. We had to be quiet, as I dared not think what the residents staying at the hotel would think about seeing two men burying something in a sack so late at night!

We returned and had a cup of tea with Mr Barrell. He then said "I'll just explain to my wife that she just died and we buried her. It'll be much better if we say that to everyone,. She'll probably go to the vets to search for another cat of course, I'll be very careful in the future."

We carried on working that night, but our thoughts remained with the accident and what had happened to that poor animal.

One Saturday morning in March, after a few hours sleep, I walked through Pontypool town to pay the rent on the TV set and I decided to take a look in the market, which was always a very busy place and was the hub of the town. The many stalls were colourful and inviting and there were always people rushing around spending their hard earned money and gossiping with friends and neighbours as they went on their way. The town was small and friendly and you could guarantee that whenever you went into the market, there would be someone there you would know. The stall holders were happy to serve the customers and business for them was always booming.

There were such shops as 'Ann's Pantry' that specialised in cooked meats and Truman's sweet stall that made their own sweets in a factory in Pontypool. Hitchin's the butchers and dozens of small stalls sold their fruit and vegetables, eggs, poultry and meat products from the nearby country farms. One of the busiest spots in the market was the café stall at the top. It was a small place that had several benches behind a wooden partition that everyone called 'The Railway Hut' as it resembled a small railway carriage. Each time I visited, it was full of people. Mr Bill Vinecombe and his wife managed it. He was a short bald headed plump man who wore spectacles that sat at the end of his nose. The couple did not have any children and were good kind hearted people who were dedicated members of the Salvation Army Mr Vinicombe's main job was in the Steelworks, but he did very well in the market as he sold the cheapest food. The small profit that he made, he donated to the Salvation Army. Mostly, everyone bought his speciality which was a large bowl of fagots and peas that he sold for a six penny piece.

While I was sat having something to eat, a school friend of mine called Tony Morgan came up and mentioned about a new 'juke box' that had recently been installed at Savinies Ice Cream Café at George Street. I always admired Tony as he was taller than me and had dark black hair which the girls always went for. He was very good looking and had the charm and charisma that anyone would be happy with.

"You ought to come along and hear it Bri, its fantastic. There are plenty of records to hear and you just put some money in and choose which one you want to hear by pressing the buttons."

"Sounds good to me, I'll go over and take a look. I haven't had much chance to get out since I started work."

"Where do you work?" he asked.

"The Carlton Bakery. I'm what you call a Bakers Boy and I work nights. How about you Tony?"

"I managed to get on the Railways. I'm engine cleaning at the moment, but training to be a fireman. There are plenty of boys from school there, you should try and come down with us, and at least it's a great future."

He seemed to insinuate that I was in a dead end job but I was happy at the bakery and declined his offer.

We both made our way to Savinies which was at the other end of town and as we approached the doorway of the café, I could see many teenagers inside dancing and jumping around. They were having a great time and I thought to myself that it was only Saturday morning. As we walked inside, the song was beginning to end and we went over to the counter and bought an ice cream each. In the corner, stood a group of teenagers surrounding something that I couldn't quite make out. "That's the juke box over there," said Tony pointing in the direction of the group. Then all of a sudden, music began to blare out and they all started shaking their heads and bodies. I thought it was quite amusing and strained to see the machine through all the activity taking place. It was bright and colourful with chrome edges and through the curved glass; you could see a record turning in the centre. When the song had ended, I asked a girl who was stood next to me who it was who had been singing. She answered "Where on earth have you been these last weeks? Have you been in a monastery?"

"I've been working since I left school last August," I replied feeling a little confused. Had I missed something very important? It struck me that I had been working so hard, I had little time to enjoy myself. John and I never seemed to go anywhere anymore and I made up my mind to put that right.

"Well, the monks have let me out now, so tell me who it is then," I answered light heartedly and she looked straight at me and said "Elvis of course!"

"Elvis who? I've never heard of the name."

"It's Elvis Presley. He's terrific," she replied.

The record was Heartbreak Hotel and when it finished, another song began and I knew immediately that it was Elvis again. This time it was Blue Suede Shoes and I thought it was even better than the first song. Everyone danced and it became addictive as without realising, my feet began tapping on the ground as well. I couldn't wait to tell John about this place and looked forward to coming back with him.

I left the café and decided to go up to Bradbury's record shop and treat myself to some new records. I hadn't bought one for a while and thought I would get an Elvis record as I still had my old wind up gramophone at home. The shop was very busy and had posters of Elvis and other new singers like

Gerry Lee Lewis and Little Richard promoting their records. Music filled the shop and Mr Bradbury was busy selling records from behind the counter. The Rock and Roll era had well and truly begun. He also sold electric record players that played up to six records that were placed on a stacker arm above a turntable. I knew I had enough money and as we had electric at home, I was eager to return and buy one. In the window, there was a dark red one, a green and a yellow one with a name plate on them saying 'Dansette' and Mr Bradbury said they were eleven pounds and came with a free record. I decided to ask Mam and Dad first to see what they thought and I rushed home hoping to get their approval. They said that they appreciated me asking them their opinion, but they said it was my money that I had worked hard for and that I could do what I wanted with it. I felt better after asking them as I never wanted to do anything they may have disapproved of.

That evening, John and I went to the cinema and I stayed over at his house as I did most Saturdays. I was so excited about telling John about the juke box, the new rock and roll sounds and the new record player I was going to buy. The next day, we set off for Savinies café to listen to the juke box and after a few songs; he became a keen rock and roll fan and especially liked Elvis. John was still at school, so I told him to come over to my house on Monday evening after work and listen to my new record player.

Chapter 14

Bitter Disappointment

After work on Monday morning, I went home to bed and awoke at around 2 o'clock in the afternoon. I collected the money from Lloyds bank for the new record player from Bradbury's Record shop and bought the maroon coloured set from the window. They gave me a free record which was Elvis' Heartbreak Hotel and I bought another rock and roll record, Bill Haley's 'See You Later Alligator'. I hurried home to hear them.

Later that evening, John came to our house to see my new player and we listened to my records. Derek and Susan stood watching and were fascinated by the turntable spinning around and the record stack changing on its own. As I was sorting the records, I noticed that my hands looked strange. They suddenly looked very old and Derek said that they looked like sand paper. I began to feel very anxious as they began to itch badly, and I felt like I had to hide them away in case anyone commented on how bad they looked.

I went on to buy Elvis' record Hound Dog and Blue Suede Shoes and in March, I bought his first album, which was the first to reach one million copies sold.

That July, a universal love story began to emerge and was shown on television. It was the marriage of Hollywood film star Grace Kelly to Prince Rainier of Monaco. We also received the bad news that Egypt had seized the Sues Canal and by November, petrol rationing came into force.

1956 and we enjoyed a great summer. John sold petrol from the pumps and Mike Taylor was still working as a trainee mechanic for Norman Jenkins. We still enjoyed visiting Cardiff regularly on the weekends to see the theatre shows. We saw American singing stars such as Tony Bennett, Slim Whitman, Billy Daniels and Johnnie Ray. We also went to the Motor Show at Earls Court with Mr Barrell, travelling up to London by train and saw Lady Dockers Car on show with its gold plated door handles.

By November of this year, the condition of my hands had deteriorated rapidly and I could no longer hide them away. Dad demanded that I visit the doctor as he had made an appointment for me the following day. I explained to Mr Barrell that I had to go and he looked very disappointed but agreed that I needed to go and seek some advice. I went along to Mount Pleasant Surgery at Pontypool and the doctor examined my hands and said "I understand that you work at the Carlton Bakery, Brian."

"Yes doctor that's right. It's behind the Clarence Hotel."

"I know its owner Edgar Barrell, a friend of mine. I'm sorry Brian but you won't be able to work with flour anymore," he said shaking his head.

"What do you mean I can't work with flour? I have to go to work tonight and I can't let my boss down."

"I don't know about that son," he said lifting his shoulders. "You have an industrial disease called dermatitis and I would say without hesitation that you have contracted this as you are allergic to flour. It's extremely uncommon but it does happen in rare cases and unfortunately it has happened to you. You will have to cover your hands with a special cream every day and completely cover them with bandages."

"How long will it take before they get better doctor?"

He shrugged his shoulders and said that it would probably take about three to six months to clear and even then it would most likely leave some scarring. He said that they were in a very bad state and I should have come along to see him earlier.

"Do you mean to tell me that I won't be able to work in the bakery until then?"

"That is up to you and your employer, but it will undoubtedly return if you handle flour on a regular basis. Obviously I will state on your sick note that you have an industrial disease and this will give you slightly more sickness benefit."

To make sure of the diagnosis, he called another doctor to look at my hands and he agreed that I did have dermatitis.

The words that were spoken to me seemed to come from someone speaking through a thick freezing fog. I felt numb and bitterly disappointed. I never thought that I would no longer be working for Mr Barrell. Maybe it was a little denial on my part but I really could not take it in. The realisation hit as he began writing and completing forms, occasionally glancing at me as I sat there in silence. He could see how upset I was at the thought of never being able to return to work at the bakery. He handed me some forms and a prescription and said that he wanted to see me in a month's time.

I came out of the surgery in a daze and walked slowly home thinking how Mr Barrell was going to manage that night without me. How was I going to tell him that I probably could not work for him anymore?

I arrived home where Mam and Dad sat waiting anxiously for me. Dad had been on his rounds, but had called home to hear the results of the doctor's diagnosis. I sat down with the forms in my hands and looked at them both before bursting into tears.

"What's happened son? Why are you so upset?" asked Dad, as he put his arm around me and took the forms from my hands.

"Now what's this? Dermatitis?" he said in a quiet voice. "That's a disease isn't it?"

Rubbing the tears away, I sobbed and told them what the doctor had said. They looked very upset for me but said they weren't surprised.

"We knew your hands were bad Brian, but we didn't think it was from the bakery," Mam said as she read the prescription.

"What am I going to do Dad? I should be working tonight and I just can't go and let Mr Barrell down."

"We'll have to contact him and tell him the situation is not your fault. He'll understand. Now don't upset yourself any more," Dad said as he wiped the tears from my face.

"I know but I can't help it. The thought of me telling him that I can't work for him anymore is awful. You know how much the bakery means to me, what will I do? I will have to work somewhere else now."

"Well Brian, it's one of those things in life that you can do nothing about. You have your health and strength, let's get your hands better first and then we will see what happens. I'll go over to Mr Barrel's house and tell him the outcome of your visit to the doctor and that you won't be able to work tonight. It will give him the chance to make some other arrangements."

"Thanks Dad. Tell him I will see him tomorrow morning. You will come back and tell me what he said won't you?"

Mam went off to the chemist to collect the prescription and the bandages and Dad came back a little later and explained that Mr Barrell said he knew several men he could call upon at any time to work for him and that I wasn't to worry about anything. He said he would see me in the morning. Dad then went off to work on his rounds and I felt much better knowing that Mr Barrell would be alright but I dreaded having to go and see him the next morning.

My mother returned with the cream and bandages and covered my hands I could see how difficult it would be working anywhere with my hands like this and how impossible it would be to handle the flour in the bakery.

Moments later, Mam went off to do some shopping and I drifted off to sleep in the chair. It was around midday and I had been working all night and felt overwhelmingly tired. I awoke several hours later to hear Derek and

Susan's voices as Mam had collected them from school. They looked surprised to see me, as I was usually in bed at that time of the day. "Why is our Brian asleep in the chair?" asked Susan, as she climbed and snuggled into my arms as she usually did whenever I sat down. "What are those bandages for?" She said looking up at my face as I slowly awoke.

Derek stood looking with a frown on his face wondering what was happening and he also asked what was wrong with me and why I wasn't in bed?

My mother stood and folded her arms and explained that I wouldn't be going to work that night as I had something wrong with my hands. She said that they were covered in cream to make them better.

Susan asked if they would be better tomorrow as she held my hand closely. I said they would take a while to get better as I held onto her tight and hid my sad feelings. That evening, I took both of them to Pontypool Park as I often did and later I took them up to bed and told them a story before they went to sleep.

As I lay in bed, I felt insecure as I looked down at my bandaged hands above the bed clothes. I went over the past day and wondered how I would feel after I had visited Mr Barrell. I also wondered what job I would do when my hands were better. As we shared the same bedroom, I looked over at my brother and sister and remembered that Christmas was only a few weeks away. I hoped I would have enough money left over to buy them a Christmas present after I had paid my mother for my keep.

The next morning my mother changed the cream and bandages and I took Derek and Susan to school. I then made my way up to the bakery. The lights were on, so I knew that Mr Barrell was still there. I had difficulty opening the bakery door with my bandaged hands and I felt that I had no right to be there anymore. A horrible feeling of being unwanted came over me. I walked in as he was getting a tray of cakes out of the oven. I thought he looked pale and he had beads of sweat trickling down the sides of his face. He glanced over at me with a sad look and then smiled and said "hello Brian, I won't be a minute. Put the kettle on, I could do with a cup of tea."

My hands were shaking slightly as I filled the kettle and got the cups and teapot ready. I poured the tea and sat down. He came over wiping his hands and face in a cloth and he ruffled my hair as he sat opposite me looking very tired.

"Hello son and how are you?" he said in a warm reassuring voice and glancing at my hands.

"Well okay I guess," I said with a slight smile lifting my hands. "You got the message from Dad then?"

"Yes thanks. I'm glad you let me know straight away Brian."

"I was very disappointed about not coming in, but you managed alright then?"

"Yes of course we did. I called a man who lives near me who's not working. Obviously it was a bit difficult as Graham and I had to show him the ropes but we managed alright." He then spoke in a genuine sincere voice. "Anyway that's enough about work. It's you that's important."

I sat in silence for several seconds that seemed to last for hours. I struggled to catch my breath and spoke as if I was exhausted.

"I expect you appreciate that I probably won't be able to return to work for you again." I struggled to say the words and looked down at my hands. The enormity of the disappointment I felt overwhelmed me.

"I know Brian; I expected it when your father told me about what the doctor had said. I had previously suspected it, but I couldn't be the one to tell you. I'm very sorry for you and if I could keep you here, I would but as you know, it's impossible because of the flour."

As he spoke, tears began to well in my eyes and I tried as best as I could to wipe them away.

"I loved it here with you and Graham and the years I worked for you before I left school. What'll you do now I've finished?"

"Now don't concern yourself. Listen; if it's any consolation, I am going to tell you something confidential. In the last few weeks, I have been talking to Mrs Barrell. I'm getting on in years and don't really want to work nights and with the sad thought that you will be finishing working for me, I may decide to end baking bread altogether. It's getting more costly to produce and I could buy in bulk from one of the big bakeries like Avana or Reece's. It's almost as cheap and I can still supply my customers and I will continue making cakes and pastries myself. I spoke to Graham about it last night and he's happy to go back to working days. Oh and by the way, Graham was very upset to hear about your hands and he wants you to call and see him."

I was surprised to hear what he said but I knew it made sense. I felt a little pleased after he explained and confided in me about his plans.

"Mrs Barrell sends her love and will miss you very much. She said you're always welcome to call in and see us. I also wish you all the best and hope your hands will be better soon. I'm sure you will get another job, you're so willing! If you want a reference at any time, just tell them to contact me. Well, I'm going home now Brian. It's been a busy night and I'm so tired. Call in and see us, mind, if it's only to make the tea! In the meantime, I'll sort out your employment documents and whatever money you're entitled to."

"Thank you Mr Barrell. I feel so much better now."

With that he stood up, shook my hand and put his other arm around my shoulder. I began to fill up again. "Bye Mr Barrell, see you soon," I said as I left quickly before any more tears appeared.

A few months later, the bakery ended baking bread but continued in business for many years until Mr Barrell retired and went to Monmouth to live. When the ovens were taken out, the bakery became a car repair workshop for Norman Jenkins's son Richard.

John and I continued to be great friends and we went everywhere together including the cinema. We were so excited when Elvis' first film 'Love Me Tender' was shown early in December. In the film, he was conveyed as a country boy during the American Civil War which was a far cry from the rock and roll singer we knew him to be. It was great to see the film on the big screen.

Christmas came and I managed to buy everyone a present with the money that I had saved. The New Year came and went and most days I helped Dad with his rounds, knocking on doors to pass away the days. I pondered my future and hoped my hands would recover soon as they were still in a pretty bad state.

January 1957 began with the resignation of Prime Minister Anthony Eden over the failure to re-secure the seized Suez Canal. His replacement was Harold Macmillan.

By February, my hands began to show signs of improvement and by the end of March; they were looking normal except for some scares. After a visit to the doctor, they agreed that the condition had cleared and I was so thankful. How lovely it was to discard those bandages. John and I celebrated and went to Cardiff for the day to see the British rock and roll singer Tommy Steele in the evening. My mind was already racing with thoughts about where I could begin a new job. It did worry me that as I was over sixteen years old, I was too old to start an apprenticeship and I did not have any certificates of education or qualifications. John was now fifteen and working as a full time apprentice mechanic for Norman Jenkins Michael Taylor had finished working for Norman and had started working down the coal mines. It occurred to me that perhaps I would land up working down the mines but I didn't want to as I seen enough of my father coming home covered in coal dust.

Chapter 15

Great Western Railways

Just south of Pontypool, the Great Western railway had a large depot where offices, maintenance and cleaning departments were stationed. Firemen and drivers were also based there. It was all housed in a very large black dirty building called 'the shunting sheds' and was surrounded by miles of railway tracks dotted with steam engines of all shapes and sizes, moving and shunting trucks around which were usually laden with coal.

The Railways were one of the largest employers in the area and a number of my friends worked there and seemed happy enough. I enquired about the possibility of becoming a fireman on the steam engines. However, I was informed that before you could become a fireman, you had to work as an engine cleaner. The system worked in a seniority way with the longest serving cleaner obtaining the next fireman's vacancy. It worked the same way for drivers, with the most senior fireman becoming the next driver when a vacancy arose. On average, you would do about six months engine cleaning, during which time you would do around two weeks training as a fireman. You would then begin work on the small shunting engines and local valley lines until you became more experienced and then you moved onto the larger express trains.

As I had no option, I decided to try and join the Railways. I applied by letter and was informed that I had to attend a medical examination in Swindon. The outcome was a success and I received a letter of confirmation that I could begin work as an engine cleaner with a view to become a fireman when a vacancy occurred.

On Monday the 1st of April 1957, I began the early morning shift at 6am. I cycled to the 'sheds' and reported in at the clocking-in office. Two other boys also started that morning, but as they were slightly older than me I was informed that they were higher in seniority. We were each given a disk which had a different number on it. All employees had one and mine displayed the number 397.

You collected your disk at the beginning of each shift and handed it back into the office when your work was finished for the day. It was hung on a large board for everyone to know who was on duty just by glancing at the particular numbers on the disks.

Bill Williams was the foreman over at the cleaners and he was also an ex-engine driver. A chubby sweaty man with a small black moustache, he looked like a very old version of Oliver Hardy. He showed us to the store room where we collected our uniforms which were dark blue bibs and brace overhauls, a little jacket and plastic peaked cap that looked like the ones the New York Police officers wore.

We were then shown around the main shed a large dark black building with a big turntable at the centre on which a steam engine would drive to be turned to the correct position for the nearest empty bay. Here it would be cleaned or repaired by the maintenance men.

We then visited the 'cleaner's cabin', a small dingy black iron and tin building. Smoke filled the inside from a cast iron coal fire. There were a few dirty benches and

Tables scattered around where the cleaners had their tea breaks and this would be where we were stationed in between jobs. There were around six cleaners on each shift of 6am until 2pm and 2pm until 10pm. We were told to put on our overhauls and wait there until we were collected and so we sat here and chatted to one another amidst the clouds of smoke.

The two lads with me were Billy Roberts from Abergavenny and Keith Felton from Cwmbran. We became very good friends. We fitted and adjusted our new working clothes and began to have a bit of a laugh as Billy did his impersonation of the actor Rod Stiger and I had a go at impersonating the Forman as Oliver Hardy. Billy was well built with a mop of curly hair. He was a motor bike scrambler enthusiast while Keith was very fair headed, gentle and quiet.

Not long after, a cleaner called in on us and we were told to follow him as the foreman was waiting for us. We walked with him and chatted while we went into the large dark turntable shed. In the corner of the building, we could just make out the foreman amid the smoke and smuts. He stood next to a large wooden box and issued us with a pile of cleaning rags and a bucket with a kind of thin oil inside. We were shown to a large green and brass steam engine that was parked in one of the bays. It was filthy dirty and covered in smuts and grime. The foreman instructed the other cleaners to show us what to do and what to clean, then explained that every train had a different number and when he wanted an engine cleaned, he would call out that number. This was unless the engine had a name, as did the one we stood glancing at. He stood proudly with his shoulders back and said "This gentleman is the pride of our fleet. It's our best steam engine. Every depot has its favourite and this is ours. This is the one we take our pride in."

I glanced at him in a confused state and thought that it didn't do much for me. I thought it looked like any other dirty scruffy engine. I thought it was only a steam engine and that he must be mad as I couldn't have cared less. I didn't want to clean it anyway, I had heard that people who worked on these engines became addicted and thought nothing else mattered. I really couldn't understand what the fuss was about. He wandered around to the side of the engine and pointed up at the name plate which read 'Hazely Grange' and displayed the number 6,8,40. I thought this was a coincidence as it was my date of birth, but still I did not feel thrilled. I carried on with the cleaning job and carried out my task diligently. All the other cleaners seemed to enjoy their work but I didn't like it at all.

I did some theory fireman training at Cardiff, which was about warning lights and what to do in an emergency and how to get as much 'steam up' as possible from the engine boiler. The subject continued to bore me and I wished I could have done something different like our John and become a mechanic or better still, I wished I could return to the bakery.

Every depot had a 'call boy' on each shift that was stationed in the offices. His duties were lighting the office fire and the fire in the Shed Masters office. He would also go by train to Newport and deliver important paperwork. But his main duty was to go to the homes of any driver or fireman and inform them when they were required to be on duty. This job had to be carried out every day so one of the conditions was that they had to work every day of the week. In between jobs, the call boy would sit on a stool and collect and give out the 'on duty' discs. He was always chosen from the engine cleaners who usually volunteered for the job. Most cleaners didn't like it in the office as it meant mixing with the management and clerks, but if no one volunteered, the job would go to the most senior cleaner.

At the beginning of an afternoon shift one day in June, the foreman came into the cabin and announced in a firm voice that the current call boy Johnny Morris had been made up to a fireman and the office manager Mr Govan had asked him to find a replacement. There was silence for a few moments and then he looked over to Keith Felton and said that if none of us volunteered, Keith would have to take the job as he was the most senior among us. He explained that he didn't think Keith would be doing the job for too long as he was next in line to become a fireman. Keith shrugged his shoulders and said that he didn't really want the job, but if no-one wanted it then he would do it. I sat there taking in the scene and it flashed through my mind that there would be no more cleaning and the extra money working weekends would be welcome. I took my chance, stood up and said to Mr Williams that I would be happy to do it. All the boys gazed up from across the tables and I glanced over to Keith who looked very pleased. "Thanks Brian, you really have done me a favour as the thought of being in those offices makes me shudder!"

"I don't mind, it doesn't bother me," I answered.

The foreman interrupted and asked if I was sure that I wanted to take on the role and asked me if I knew what the job entailed. I replied that I had spoken to Johnny as we travelled to work together sometimes as he was from Pontypool. "Well, that's it then Brian, the job's yours until you're made up as fireman which should hopefully be in about six month's time. Collect your haversack and tea urn and follow me to the offices to see the office manager."

"See you all again!" I said to the boys, as they wished me all the best. I was pleased as I walked along with the foreman through the dark sheds until we came to a brightly lit long corridor. The walls were covered with large sheets of names and off-duty times for the firemen and drivers as they came on and off duty at different times. We came to the office door and stepped inside. Mr Williams took off his cap and fiddled with his hands. He stood silently and attempted to look important. I gazed across the large room at the clerks who were sat at their desks. They had shaded lights hanging above their heads from the ceiling and they all looked up at us over their spectacles.

To my left, I noticed an empty stool positioned in front of the window. One of the clerks whispered to a man sat behind a large desk in the far corner. He looked up and then nodded his head towards Mr Williams who tapped his cap against my arm, gesturing me to walk forward with him. "Hello Mr Govan, this is Brian Jenkins, the new call boy that you requested. He volunteered for the job and I'm sure he will do a fine job. He's from Pontypool." He leaned back in his chair and looked up at me. I stood there with my haversack over my shoulder feeling very uneasy and a little intimidated. He was a tall grey haired man with a dignified air about him.

"Yes I've seen Brian before, throwing his disk in with the other cleaners. Leave him with me Bill, I'll sort him out" and with that, the foreman left clutching his cap.

"Right son, my name is Gorvan, as you probably know and I'm the office manager. These gentlemen sat around us are our friends. Well, some are!"

he said jokingly. The clerks lifted their heads and looked around at me. "This is Brian, our new call boy and he's starting today."

They all muttered a welcome and carried on working. "Firstly, you need to light the fires in here and in the shed master's office. You don't have to wear your cap and overhauls in the offices. There's a small locker under this desk where you can keep them. You may need them in the unlikely event that you may be called upon to do a firing turn on the weekend. Is that alright with you?"

"Yes of course, sir. The sooner the better really, so I know what it's like."

He walked over to the enquiry window and pulled the stool from under the counter. "Sit here Brian and give out these disks." He pointed to a large board which was covered with numbered hooks and disks hanging from them. "When an employee comes on duty and calls his number, hand him his disk and when his shift is over, he will hand it back to you, as you know. Be sure to place it back on the same numbered hook as we can tell at a glance who is on duty and who is not. Soon enough you will learn everyone's number."

"Yes sir, that's clear enough. I was aware of the system."

"As you know, we will ask you at any time to call on any driver or fireman at their homes if we require them to come on duty. We have a bicycle in the store room if you need it, but we only call out people who live within a mile or so away."

""No trouble Mr Govan, I know the area well."

"And one other thing, some days you will need to travel by train from Pontypool Road station to Newport station offices to deliver mail. Right then, sit on your stool and read some of the books that are hanging about these desks and if you like, you can make a pot of tea for us all."

"No problem, any time gents!" I said as I climbed onto the stool and hung some of the disks that had been handed in onto the desks. The clerks were listening intently and smiled when I was asked to make the tea. I obliged happily.

I really enjoyed my time in the railways offices, even though it was only as a call boy. I got on great with everyone, although they were much older than me. When they asked where I lived, I never told them that it was down Mill Road, I just said Pontypool. I kept myself busy tidying the desks and making cups of tea especially for the shed master in his office who always had a bone china tea cup and saucer. Mr Govan and I became good friends and I used to listen to his good advice.

On the 14th of May 1957, there was much cheering in the offices as an announcement was made on the radio that petrol rationing had been abolished as it had been in force for the previous five months following the Suez crisis. The next day Britain tested its first atom bomb in the pacific on Christmas Island.

Derek was now growing up and was eight years old on the 16th of May. His leg was returning to normal after he had had it in an iron brace for the past few years after he contracted polio. Susan was six years old on the 19th of the month and I adored them both. I was so pleased that I was able to buy them each a bike for their birthdays due to me working seven days a week. I was now able to save some money, something I could not do when I was out of work with my hands so poorly.

All workers on the Railways had two free passes a year to travel anywhere in the country. With this in mind, I wrote to Aunty Marge in Newcastle-under-Lyme and asked her if she would like me to come and stay with her for a week or two during the summer holidays. She returned my letter and said that she and all the Smith family would be delighted to see me and were looking forward to my visit. She said that I could stay as long as I liked. I travelled there in June from Pontypool Road Station and I was so excited as it was the first time I had stayed away from home. I sat alone in the railway carriage and my mind drifted back to the times we shared when the family lived at Trosnant and how they helped us as we moved to Mill Road

The train arrived at Stoke on Trent and there on the platform stood Uncle George and Michael waiting for me. I was so surprised to see Michael as he looked so grown up. We hugged each other and couldn't believe it had been four years since we last saw each other. We got into a taxi and headed towards Aunty Marge's house and Uncle George showed me the coal mine where he worked as we passed through the village of Silverdale. We arrived at number 7 Stratton Row Parkside and the house looked like all the other houses around the estate, built in the Cornish style with grey roof tiles coming down to the ground floor windows. They were built especially for the coal board miners from other areas of the country. Many miners came here from South Wales, attracted by the opportunity to live in a new house.

Aunty Marge was waiting on the doorstep as we pulled up and I rushed up to her and we held each other tightly. I couldn't hold back the tears as the emotion overwhelmed me. I loved her so very much; it had been such a long time.

Cousins Jean, Esme and Mary were also there to greet me and I had another surprise as Aunty Olwyn's daughter, Elaine was visiting from London. She was also staying for the week and we had a great time with Michael, showing us around the towns of Stoke and Newcastle. It was a lovely visit and I was so glad that I made the trip. Seeing the family was special but before I knew it, I found myself giving Aunty a bunch of flowers and thanking her for my stay. I left their home with everybody waving goodbye as I made my way home again.

One Saturday evening in August, John and I went to see Elvis' new film 'Loving You' in The Park Cinema. The film portrayed him as a rock and roll singer and while we were there, we started chatting to two girls. One was called Hazel Norman and I asked her if I could take her out the following week. She accepted and I was very excited as she was the first girl I had asked out. We visited the cinema together several times and I found myself really falling for her and I thought I was in love. She was a kind and gentle girl and I always made sure that she got home safe to her parents' house every time I took her out. On one occasion, we went to Cardiff on the train with John and one of her friends, Shirley Jones. We went to see Lonnie Donnigan and his group who, at the time, had a big hit with the song 'My Old Man's a Dustman'.

A few weeks later, I went to meet Hazel outside The Royal Cinema in town. We were going to see a film with Mario Lanza called 'The Great Caruso' and as I waited, a lady approached me and asked me if my name was Brian. I said it was and she then explained that she was Hazel's mother and that Hazel would not be coming. She gave me an envelope and said it was from her daughter. I took it but didn't know what to do, so I went outside and stood in a watchmakers shop doorway where I opened it. It read:

> Dear Brian,
>
> I am sorry to tell you this and it is difficult for me as I like you very much and you have been so kind to me. I have enjoyed my time with you but I think I'm too young to have a regular boyfriend as I want to have my freedom, if that's the word. I would like to go out with my friends when I want to. I hope we can remain friends when we see one another around.
>
> Love Hazel

I was always very sensitive, but this made me feel totally lost and dejected. My thoughts were that maybe she had been put off by the fact that I lived down Mill Road. She knew where I came from as I had told her. I felt very lonely and sad as I wandered the streets in town, thinking about the times we had shared together. I didn't want to go home as I was afraid that my feelings would show, so I wandered around a little more and went into a few cafes to drink coffee. I then went off down to the Lucana billiard hall, which we called 'The Luke' for short. This was underneath the Park Cinema and was a large hall that held around eighteen tables and a small café area. It was a meeting place where men generally sat on the side and watched people play. John and I used to go there regularly and we both had our own snooker queues kept on the premises in a holder which was locked up.

I walked in and bought a cup of coffee and sat down on the side looking across at the tables. John was there with Tony Morgan and I thought how happy they looked, maybe because I was feeling so low after my letter from Hazel. I walked over to them and John asked me what I was doing there, as he thought I was out with Hazel. I said that she didn't turn up and that I would tell him about it later. I sat and watched a few games and Tony asked me to join in, but I didn't feel like it. Later, I showed John the letter and he said he was sorry as he liked Hazel. He said that he thought that maybe we were a bit young to be serious about one another and he would be glad to see more of me as I had been spending time with her and not with him. "Now listen, you're working early on Saturday so cheer up and we can go out when you finish. I'll meet you here at 3 o'clock, there's a Dean Martin and Jerry Lewis film on at the Park Cinema and we'll have a good day," he said trying to cheer me up. "Alright then, see you here on Saturday," I replied reluctantly.

We usually met in the billiard hall every Saturday and played a few games before moving on to one of the Italian Cafés for some food and then on to the cinema. We generally finished off the evening with a visit to the Queen's Ballroom which was situated in Crane Street in the centre of town. It was a very good dance hall and very popular with many famous dance bands performing.

As it was the rock and roll era, we always wore our Teddy boy clothes, which were long blue jackets, black shirts and drain pipe trousers. We learned to jive with the girls and had fun. It was the usual way of life for teenagers in the many valley towns across South Wales and Saturday nights were the highlight of the week. I slowly got over Hazel and after a few weeks, we spoke to one another a few times at the cinema. But after a few months, I never saw her again.

October 1957, the world was shocked by the news that the cold war was beginning to spread. This caused a nervous feeling and panic set in the United States of America. The Russians had launched the world's first artificial satellite called Sputnik; it was the first manmade object to leave the earth's atmosphere. The fact that it passed over the US seven times each day caused unease particularly as the rocket that launched it was capable of carrying nuclear weapons and able to launch them thousands of miles away.

I spent most of my time in the office sat on the stool reading some of the books that were scattered about the desks. There were dictionaries, phone books, maps of railway depots and maths books with algebra calculations referring to motor vehicle engines. I began to get very interested in learning these calculations of vehicle engines which was something I should have learned at Technical school. I was now realising my mistakes. By working for Dad on weekends and in the bakery after school, I missed out on studying and that affected my education. However, I never regretted this.

On November 3rd, animal welfare organisations expressed outrage as Sputnik II was launched with one passenger, a dog named Laika who was circling the planet every one hour and forty two minutes.

It was for experimental purposes and made Laika one of the world's most famous animals. Russian scientists learned much about the prospect of human space travel through the experiment.

Wednesday, 4th of December came and sadness overshadowed the whole depot as news came in of a train crash at Lewisham in London. As the horrors unfolded, everyone was saddened as the death toll rose to 94 with many hundreds injured.

Christmas came and I continued my work in the offices and wondered when my turn would come to finally become a fireman. I became discontented with the role but I did become more interested in reading about maths and calculations.

January 1958, I used my free passes to take John on a visit to London by train. We were mesmerised by the bright lights of Piccadilly and Soho and loved the city which was worlds apart from our small hometown in South Wales.

The following month, something happened that changed my perception and judgement of my future. I went to work on a Saturday afternoon and there were no cleaners on duty. All the sheds and offices were almost empty,

143

as was usually the case on weekends. I walked into the office and said hello to the two staff that were on duty and sat on the stool as the roster clerk Gethin spoke to me.

"Brian, we need a fireman on The West Bank shunting area as there are no cleaners on duty and it's too late to call a fireman out. You've had training, haven't you?"

"Yes, the theory part at Cardiff."

"Well I'm afraid you'll have to go over there now. Sorry about this, but you are my only hope."

"That's alright, that's what I'm here for. It'll give me an insight to what I'll be doing soon."

"Put your overhauls and cap on first before you go and don't forget your lunch box. Make sure you take your disk with you, it's the rules. And do as the driver tells you. His name is Les Brown."

"Thanks Gethin! I'll see you later."

It was a lovely warm afternoon and I walked out of the office and headed towards the railway lines carrying my haversack on my back. I felt proud and full of anticipation of what the next few hours would bring.

I came to the shunting yard known as "The West Bank". There were around four other sites used as well. In the centre stood a small steam engine known as a Match Box type, owing to the shape of the main body. This was surrounded by dozens of trucks stood ready to be connected to go to their correct destinations.

"Hello, Mr Brown. I'm the fireman sent over for you from the office," I shouted as I looked up at the cabin and noticed a small beaky nosed face glaring down at me from the 'footplate' area where the driver and fireman operated the engine.

"Hello son, come on up," he said. So I climbed up the steps clinging onto the rail as I hauled myself up. He pointed to a flat piece of wood sticking out of the side near the top of the steps to the left of the cabin facing the boiler door.

"Sit down there. That's your seat and this is my side," he said in firm, grumpy voice as he began pulling and pushing different levers. I did know this, but I daren't say anything.

"What's your name?"

"Brian sir, Brian Jenkins," I answered nervously.

"Haven't had you firing before for me. You new?"

"Well I'm not a regular fireman but I soon will be, as I'm second in line for a vacancy. They sent me from the office as there are no cleaners on duty today."

144

"Oh, I know who you are; you're the call boy from the office."

"Yes sir that's right."

"This must be your first firing turn?"

"Yes sir."

"Well, I guess you know what to do. Don't be afraid to ask anything, I won't bite your head off. Just keep shovelling that coal as far as you can up that boiler and keep the fire going." He paused as he looked across the yard into the distance. "This will be the only way we can hold a good head of steam," he shouted as he turned around and pointed to a long shovel that stood beside a huge pile of coal behind the foot plate, the designated coal storage area. He pointed at many trucks strewn across a wide area. "We've got to shunt all those trucks together by this evening and don't forget to keep an eye open for the guard!"

Alongside our engine, a railway guard stood, who ran along the side of the track with a long rod in his hand, to hook the chain of each truck onto one another to join them together. He would instruct the driver on which truck to shunt next and, most importantly, to look out for the stop and go signals as we approached other yards to pick up trucks.

The engine lurched forward and I almost fell out as I grabbed the hand rail. It buffed against a truck and I had difficulty standing up as there was coal all around our feet. The engine shook back and forth as it trundled around the yards. The driver shouted "You'll have to learn to hang on son!" Hang on? It was like trying to walk on an ice covered pond.

I struggled to throw the coal up into the boiler and it often landed all over the floor. The driver shouted amid the lurching and the shaking and said "Try and feed the boiler with coal when we're still!"

The shunting and buffeting continued for several hours until we came to a halt outside a little brick building at the side of the track.

As the time approached 6 o'clock, the driver informed me that it was eating time and that we ate our lunch in the mess room. He gathered his lunch box and I followed him with mine. I thought to myself I couldn't eat a thing as my stomach had turned over at least ten times. As I walked towards the building, my legs began to wobble and I suddenly felt very sick. I prayed there was a toilet in there somewhere. I entered the room and the driver and the guard were sat at a dirty coal dust covered table eating their food. The driver spoke to me as he enjoyed his thick white bread sandwich which contrasted with his black coal covered face. "Alright lad, you aint done a bad job since it's your first time. Sit down over there, I reckon we'll be finished by half past eight. You got some food with you?"

"I'm not very hungry Mr Brown, but I'm going to have some tea though," I said, as I poured myself a cup out of my flask and thought how I was going to get through another two hours of this.

He pulled another sandwich from his lunch box which was a big Oxo tin and asked if I wanted a 'sticky ass' sandwich as he had plenty of them. He thrust it towards me with jam running down his fingers. I declined politely and said that I wasn't that hungry, as I was going outside to sit down in the sunshine and if there was a toilet around. I was told it was behind a green door just outside.

Half an hour later, we returned to the engine and finished our work at 9 o'clock. I made my way across the yards to the offices and Gethin asked me how it had gone.

"Bloody marvellous for a Saturday evening, look at me!" I said, in an uncharacteristic way as I stood there covered in smuts and coal dust.

"Well, it's what you'll be doing all the time soon."

"I know Gethin, it's not your fault. It's the job that I'll be doing and that's it. It's a new week tomorrow and I'm back in the morning at 6 o'clock. I just hope there's not another firing turn awaiting me. How about you, are you on again as well?"

"Yes, I'm on at 6 as well, Brian. But don't worry, there's no need for a fireman in the morning. Why don't you go home a bit early, you deserve it?"

"I think I will. See you in the morning Gethin."

I took my overhauls off and got ready to cycle home in the dark. I felt a bit down and thought that Mam wouldn't be very happy with me going home in this dirty state. I would need a bath before I could go to bed which meant filling the tin bath with water at this late hour.

I was back in work at 6 on the Sunday morning and it was very quiet. I sat on the stool thinking about the previous evenings work as a fireman. I picked up the motor vehicle maths book I had been reading and wondered where it had come from. I began to realise that I had been wasting my time on the railway and that the job as a fireman was definitely not for me. I knew I had a long working life ahead of me and I knew in my heart that without being disrespectful to anyone working there, I could do better.

I made up my mind that from then on, I would try anything to get another job where I would be happier.

I visited the dole offices every day at Pontypool, looking for suitable vacancies but there were only jobs for labourers and apprentices at local factories for boys of 15 and 16 years old. It seemed that you needed qualifications. I was almost 18 and too old for the opportunities that were available. I also read the South Wales Argus newspaper advertisements every evening and the local Free Press to no avail. But the following Friday evening, I saw a small advert in the South Wales Argus:-

> Youth wanted 17 - 18 years old. Must be fit and strong to train as a Heavy Goods Vehicle Mechanic with a view for suitable applicants, to attend a three year City and Guild course in Motor vehicle Mechanics at the National College of Monmouthshire Crumlin.
>
> Apply to Co-ordinated Contracts, New Road, New Inn, Pontypool.

I knew exactly where the place was. I had passed it several times as it wasn't far from the railway depot. It was a vehicle repair workshop for a large fleet of blue painted Lorries hired to British Nylon Spinners who had a factory on the outskirts of Pontypool in the direction of Abergavenny.

I couldn't believe it. It was the opportunity that I wanted and I couldn't wait. I made up my mind I would go there first thing the following morning and try for the job, even if it was a Saturday. I dressed as suitably as I could and told Mam and Dad my intentions.

I cycled to New Inn and arrived at about 9 o'clock. I parked my bike outside and walked in. There were several mechanics working on vehicles inside when a man came up to me in overhauls and asked if he could help me.

I explained that I had come about the job and he answered back that he thought the manager, Mr Gilbert, was expecting people to write in. He also said that Mr Gilbert was due in shortly as he came in on a Saturday morning for a few hours before going to the Conservative Club in Pontypool.

"Do you think he'll be able to see me?" I asked.

"I don't know. Why didn't you write in for an interview?" he answered.

"Well, you know what its like, if they don't like your writing or the area you live in, they just throw your application in the bin. Why are they asking for an older trainee and not an apprentice?" I asked.

"The owner and Managing Director, Colonel Pye lives in Somerset and is an old friend of Mr Gilbert's. He wanted someone older and mature, as the job can be quite heavy."

He then looked oddly in my face and said "I think I know you. Aren't you Aubrey Jenkins' son."

"Yes, that's right I'm his oldest, Brian."

"Your dad calls on my parents with groceries; they manage the Unicorn Pub on the race road."

"Oh, I know your parents - Mr. and Mrs. Pullman? I've heard them talk of you."

"I'm Ray, Ray Pullman, and a mechanic here."

He then held out his hand, and we shook hands.

"Think your dad told me you worked on the railway?"

"Yes, that's right"

"What do you want this job for then, if you don't mind me asking."

'Well Ray, I'm lined up for a Fireman's job, but I don't like it. I've tried it and there doesn't seem to be much future in it, without being disrespectful to anyone working on the railway. Think I could do better. I'd really like to learn something in engineering - the opportunity to be a heavy goods mechanic would evidently suit me fine.   This probably could be my only chance and I would certainly relish the idea of going to a technical college."

"You do seem very interested, Brian."

"Yes my cousin John works for Norman Jenkins and my Uncle Reese works for himself repairing cars."

"Oh I know both of them - some evenings I have a drink with Reece in the bar of the Clarence. I've known him and your father for years!"

He then looked around and pointed at a mechanic working on a large engine.

"The job here is very interesting, especially building diesel engines. And of course, we have the usual breakdowns that can take you anywhere in the country."

"It gives you a wide knowledge of the routes to towns and cities. Look, I'm not saying any more in case you don't get the job and you'll be disappointed."

"Knowing my luck you're probably right! What's he like, the manager, Ray?' I asked.

"He's a grumpy old devil, smokes about 60 cigarettes a day, but don't worrym he's alright. I don't think he's bothered who he employs, he's retiring in a year or two and only employing a trainee on the orders of the colonel."

Just then a green Ford Prefect car pulled up outside and parked. A short elderly man in a dark grey suit stumbled out carrying a brief case. He walked towards us.

"Morning Mr Gilbert," Ray shouted.

"Morning. Everything alright, Ray?" he muttered.

"Yes, no problems, Mr Gilbert."

He then turned around and walked towards the stairs that led up to the offices that overlooked the Workshops, and then Ray spoke again.

"Oh, sorry to bother you, Mr Gilbert, but there's a lad here, he's called in about the trainee job advertised in the South Wales Argus."

"He's anxious, isn't he? Didn't expect anyone to call in here, especially on a Saturday morning." he answered, in a crispy voice, as he carried on walking towards the stairs.

I walked away silent and nervous, thinking maybe I'd blown my chance and should have written in.

"What shall I do with him then Mr Gilbert? Tell him to write in?" Ray asked. "He seems a nice lad, and very appreciated of the opportunity."

He then stopped, put his briefcase down on the steps and pulled a packet of cigarettes from his pocket. He handed one to Ray and lit one himself.

In a haze of smoke, he glanced over at me, behind his brown glasses.

My heart was in my mouth, thanking Ray under my breath for what he said.

"Well I'm not very busy this morning, Ray. I suppose, since he's made the effort to come here this morning, I could have a word with him in my office. I'll send down for him in about half an hour."

Ray looked over to me and said, "Is that all right with you?"

"Yes Ray, thanks," I answered nervously.

I looked across at the manager. I was too far away to see his features properly as he picked his briefcase up and turned to go upstairs. I shouted over loudly.

"Thank you very much, sir."

He didn't answer, only gave a nod as he slowly walked up the stairs.

"Come in the tea room and have a cup of tea while you wait," Ray said.

We walked into a room underneath the offices. It was all very clean and tidy.

In the centre stood a large oblong table with six chairs around it. Two more chairs were near the window.

A lovely man with a pleasant face aged about 65 years old got up from his seat and switched on a water boiler near a kitchen sink.

"Dai, make this lad a cup of tea. He's waiting to see George about that job."

"Brian, this is Dai Cook, he's our tea maker and pump man. He refuels all the vehicles when they arrive in. He'll look after you."

"Hello, Mr Cook, nice to meet you," I said as I sat down at the table.

"Hello son, how are you? Where you from then?" he asked, as he was brewing a pot of tea.

"I live in Pontypool, near Clarence Street, you know the road leading into Pontypool town?"

"I know, I lived up there once, on Broadway. We moved to the Highway in New Inn years ago."

"You've not far to come then, Mr Cook?"

"No, only down over the hill, about five minutes away," he said as he handed me a cup of tea.

"Listen son, the mechanics will be in here soon to have their break. Don't sit on any of the chairs at the table as the mechanics each have their own seat. The one chair by the window is Ken, the painter's seat, so sit on the other one by the window. And by the way, we only call Mr Gilbert "George" among ourselves," he said, with a devilish grin.

"I guessed that, Mr Cook! I'll wait outside, I don't mind."

"No, no, son, it's alright. It's only when they all come in together. It's quicker anyway as they have their own tea cup put ready in front of them.'

I went over and sat by the window.

"I understand Mr Cook," I said, still wondering why it was so regimental.

I felt so much at home sat there chatting to the tea man, or whatever he was.

He was so friendly, and Ray had been so helpful and the thought of returning to be a Fireman on the railway really dampened my spirits.

But then my thoughts turned to the Manager in the office above me. It seemed like a black cloud hovering above my head, waiting to burst before a thunder storm, and wondering, would he be horrible and resentful towards me? What was he going to ask me about?

The tea room door opened and Ray looked over at me.

"You can go upstairs. He's ready to see you now."

My hands began to shake as I put the cup I was holding on the table.

"Good luck, son," Mr Cook said.

I came out of the tea room, just as a bell rung for the of start of their tea break. All the mechanics then passed me and headed into the tea room.

I took a deep breath, went upstairs and strode into the first large open offices.

I passed a man sat at a desk who nodded at me. His name was L Tredgold, who was evidently the routing clerk as his name and position was written on a large plaque on his desk.

I then came to an office girl, sat behind a desk typing.

"I'm to see Mr Gilbert," I said.

She smiled up at me and pointed at a door a few yards further with a big name plate 'Mr. G Gilbert' written on it. She spoke quietly. "That's his office. He's ready to see you now."

I felt very nervous, my heart started beating fast. It was the first time I ever had an interview of any kind.

I tapped on the door and a throaty voice answered. "Come in."

I entered and the first thing I encountered was the smell coming from the smoke filled room.

Amidst the smoke behind a desk sat Mr Gilbert stubbing out a cigarette, into a large tray filled with ash. He was a round-faced, balding man, with large puffy eye bags showing under his spectacles. He looked at me and mumbled,

"Well, you've come about the job then?"

"Yes Sir, I have."

His voice then changed gruffly "Sit down then. Tell me, why you didn't write in? I didn't expect anyone simply to call in."

"Well Sir, I'm sorry to cause you any trouble, but I thought if I wrote in, I might not get an interview."

"What makes you think you wouldn't get one?"

I shrugged my shoulder and answered "I don't know. All I know is, I'm really desperate for a job where I can learn something and better myself, and this job seems just the opportunity I was I hoping to find."

He smiled and seemed pleased with what I had said.

He lit another cigarette and amid the smoke with his nicotine-covered fingers, he held a note book to his face. He obvious had difficulty reading the words because of his eyesight and started reading something from it.

"I've got to ask you some questions. What type of school did you attend?"

"A Technical school, sir. Abersychan Technical School."

I then prayed that he wouldn't ask me about any qualifications.

"What did you do when you left school?"

"Worked in a bakery, sir."

"Why did you stop working there?"

I paused and said "Unfortunately, I contracted a skin disease from the flour and had to finish, but it's cleared, I'm alright now."

"Are you working now?"

"Yes sir. I'm on the railways at the moment, but unfortunately, I don't think there's any future for me. It's a fireman's job. However, if I'm unsuccessful in getting this job, I'll search until I find something else. I won't give up."

"This is the first time we've employed a young person as a trainee."

He then read from the note book. "All applicants must understand the agreement and whoever is successful in obtaining the vacancy must sign it. First you've got to attend a Technical college next September, for at least a three year course in motor vehicle mechanics. If at the end you fail to come up to our standard or fail to obtain any City and Guild qualification or fail to hold a full driving license by the time you are twenty one, we have the right to, at our discretion, cease to employ you any further. If on the other hand the trainee is successful in all these items, then a position as a first class vehicle Technician will be established, for him at any of our numerous branches, situated across the country." With that, he paused and took a draw on his cigarette again.

"I don't think there's anything else I've got to say. Is that all clear to you?"

"Certainly Mr Gilbert."

"Have you got any thing else to say, son?"

I was taken back slightly as he called me 'son' and I felt much easier.

"Well sir, if given this unexpected opportunity and coupled with my interests in maths and mechanics, I'm sure I won't let myself, or anybody else down. I will do the very best I can for you and your company."

With that, he stood up and drew on his cigarette and said sharply, "Give the girl outside your name and address before you go."

Then in a quiet friendly voice muttered, "thank you for calling in. We'll let you know."

"Thank you very much," I answered as I left the office.

He closed the door behind me. I looked at my watch - I had only been in there about eight minutes. It seemed ages.

I stood in front of the girl. She was only about twenty years old, pretty with fair hair. She whispered "How did you get on?"

I whispered back "He's a bit abrupt isn't he? He told me to give you my name and address, but I don't think much of my chances though, somebody with some fancy exam results will probably get the job."

She smiled again and whispered "Don't be concerned, he's like that with everybody. He's alright really, except he smokes too much. He's a cockney from London, lives on his own in Cwmbran."

She then wrote my name and address down and wished me good luck as I left.

I came down the stairs and walked towards my bike parked outside, when came Ray over to me.

"Alright?" he asked.

"Well I suppose so. I'll just have to wait and see. I'm on afternoons today and I haven't had any breakfast yet, I was too pensive to eat anything this morning."

"Listen, I'll try and put a good word in for you, Brian, if I can, but no promises, ok?"

"Well, thanks Ray. That's good of you. Remember me to your mam and dad," I replied, as I got on my bike and rode away, feeling a little despondent. I returned home and later went to work that afternoon.

The next two weeks I waited impatiently for a reply but nothing arrived. I looked again in the local newspapers and went to the Labor Exchange, still hoping to find a suitable vacancy, but to no avail.

It was now three weeks since I had been interviewed at Co-ordinated, and I began to accept the fact I wouldn't be getting the job, and that I would be staying on the Railway for some time.

Compulsory two-year National Service was still in operation, but the government was considering bringing it to an end, but if not, maybe I would be 'called up' for the army when I became 18 years old in August; I really was at a crossroads.

Early the next week, I returned home from a morning shift at about half past two in the afternoon. There was nobody at home; my mother had gone out early to Porthcawl for the day with Derek and Susan.

Susan had been suffering from a bad whooping cough and the doctors suggested she should try breathing in fresh sea air as it might help.

I opened the front door and on the floor was an envelope the postman had delivered earlier. It read 'Mr B Jenkins, 14 Mill Road, Pontypool.'

I was surprised, as I never received much post and so wondered what it might be. I sat down and opened it and started reading. It was from Co-ordinated Contracts.

Co-ordinated Contracts
New Road
New Inn
Pontypool
February 1st 1958

Dear Mr Jenkins

We are sorry for the delay in responding to your recent interview. We had to supply our Managing Director with all the details of each applicant, and obviously as he has been away on holiday, there was a time delay. I am sorry to cause you undue anxiety.

After giving all applicants considerable thought between ourselves, we are pleased to offer you the vacancy of trainee Mechanic.

If you are still willing to except this appointment, please call here and sign the necessary documents. Please bring your birth certificate with you.

Obviously, we know you'll have to give your present employer their required notice to start work with us, so that we can then come to an agreement on the date you can begin with us

Yours faithfully
G .Gilbert

I sat down, I couldn't believe it! I was absolutely bowled over, my hopes had gone completely about obtaining the job.

Tears came to my eyes, as I felt a sense of apprehension at the thought of going to college and the expectations of me, but it was the first major break I'd had and I knew I would be giving it my best effort.

I ran over to Norman's garage and told our John of my good news.

He was delighted and enjoyed the fact that the both of us would be starting at the Technical College together next September. Later that day, I showed my parents the letter. They were so pleased for me to have this chance of better future prospects.

The next morning I handed in my notice at the Railway office.

I was really surprised, the office staff and engine cleaners seemed so pleased for me.

The office manager gave me the maths and calculations book which had belonged to him, as a farewell gift.

Later that day, I cycled to the Co-ordinated Depot and thanked Mr Gilbert for offering me the vacancy. I signed the necessary papers and agreed to start in two weeks. I left the building with such an air of excitement and expectation.

That week I bought two new pairs of dark blue overhauls and a new pair of working shoes to begin my new job.

I completed my notice on the railway on the afternoon shift of February 6th. It was late evening and I sat on the office stool, hanging the disks on the board. All the staff had gone home. Gethin put his radio on and while listening, news came through that seven Manchester United footballers were among twenty one dead, after an air crash at Munich airport. I was shocked and upset as I was beginning to take an interest in football, especially Manchester United.

The British European Airways plane had caught fire shortly after takeoff with thirty eight passengers and six crew.

The aircraft was bringing the team and entourage back from a European cup match in Yugoslavia and had stopped to re-fuel in Munich.

The football world reeled at such a loss of such talented players, whose average age was only twenty four.

The Queen said she was deeply shocked and sent a message to the Mayor of Manchester.

Chapter 16

Loss of Innocence

I arrived at Co-ordinated on February 18th 1958 to start work at 8 o'clock. The first person for me to see in the tearoom was Dai Cook.

I remember his distinct words.

"Hello, young Brian. Glad you got the job. I'm sure you'll do all right, son."

"Thank you, Mr Cook. I'm glad too."

"By the way, your clock card is in the rack, next to the clock. It's number eight. All the staff 'clock on'. By the way, call me Dai from now on, son."

"Ok then, Dai," I said, with a grin as I went out to 'clock on'.

Just then, Ray came in and I thanked him for putting in a good word.

"Don't thank me; I think you impressed the old man with your enthusiasm," he answered.

I then went into the tearoom, sat down and started putting my overhauls on. Dai pointed outside through the window at cars pulling up outside in the car park and informed me who the fitting staff were as they arrived.

The first to appear were two middle aged men in an old Austin 10 car.

"That's the two Ronnies, from Aberbeeg," Dai said. Then a Morris 8 pulled up. "That's Roy Morris, the foreman, and Ron Moyle, the tyre fitter, both from Abergavenny."

"You've plenty of Ronnies working here," I said to Dai.

"Yes, they're all head cases!" he answered, with a joking grin.

Then in walked two men. Dai introduced me to them both, Ken Kilminster, the painter from nearby Griffistown and fitter's mate, Jack Knight from Cwmbran.

They all wished me well and after they had all put on their overhauls, they departed onto the workshops to carry on with their duties.

The foreman Roy Morris, a pleasant blond haired man of about thirty, began to show me around the premises.

In the centre, three large long 'pits' sank into the ground with steps at each end. The vehicles parked over them to enable the maintenance staff to maintain them from underneath.

He showed me the stores where the spare parts were kept and the paint shop where Ken the painter hand painted the vehicles when required.

Outside there was a large parking area with two filling pumps, one petrol and one diesel.

Roy explained there were fifty vehicles and twenty trailers of all different makes and they were all serviced on a mileage basis.

The next few weeks, I fitted in very well and made good progress. I was assigned to Ray Pullman, who first taught me all about vehicle servicing systems.

Ray was smart man with wavy fair hair; he was a regular drinker in the Pubs of Pontypool. His wife sadly had died recently.

All mechanics bought their own hand tools and kept them in their own tool boxes. Ray explaining to me which types I needed, so I began buying my own and slowly building up my own collection.

All the mechanics were great characters, especially the two Ronnies and fitter's mate, Ron Williams, known as 'Little Ron' as he was only 5 feet tall. His travelling mate was mechanic Ron Powell, nicknamed 'Tosha' because he had a long handlebar moustache.

Ron Powell played the saxophone every evening in different pubs and drank like a fish. His hands were always shaking from the affects of alcohol.

During the day, he would go down the pit under the vehicles and started rolling his own cigarettes and filling a tin box to save him rolling his own in the evening.

Due to his hand shaking, he was a hopeless mechanic. It was only because he was a lovable character and a good friend to everybody he kept his job.

The other Ron was Ron Moyle, the tyre fitter.

Jack Knight from Cwmbran was the one who greased all the vehicles. When they were due for a service, he was always known as 'grease monkey Jack'. He always wore a greasy cap but he was a good mate to have on a cold day on a breakdown.

He was as hard as nails, he never felt the cold A mass of black curly hair bulged out from his chest, from a wide-open shirt in all weathers conditions.

The only problem with Jack was that his feet always smelt. I always put it down to the onions he ate. He would eat a large whole onion in his tea break twice a day, just like anyone would eat an apple.

He always said "I eat them to keep me fit and strong."

I used to say "You may be right, but we have to be fit and strong to put up with your smelly feet!" We always remained good friends and he never took any notice of what I said.

After a few months, the foreman, Roy, and his mate Ron from Abergavenny finished working with us and were replaced by a mechanic named Tommy Wakefield, and fitters mate Paddy Atkins. Tom was a first class fitter, although he was deep and secretive. He was my idol, so smart with jet black hair.

Over the next few months, I applied for a learner's driving license and began driving lorries around the yard. By June, I began to think about buying a cheap car.

One Saturday night out with John, we were chatting in the billiard hall and he told me Norman Jenkins had a car for sale. A 1938 Morris 8.

"How much is he asking for it?"

"I think he wants forty pounds for it, but I'm not sure."

He had set my mind thinking. I had saved over that amount in the bank and would love a car of my own.

"Let's go and have look at it in the morning. Will you come with me?" I asked John.

"Are you serious? You've not passed your test yet anyway. Can you afford it then?" he answered.

"Just about, if it's under forty pounds. I'll be applying for my driving test soon. Is Norman there on a Sunday?"

"Yes, in the morning. I'll come with you, but don't quote me about the price, I may be wrong."

Outside the workshop in New Inn 1958. Rear, Jim Rice, Me, Ray Pullman, Paddy Atkins. Front – Ron Powell, Ron Williams, Tom Wakefield

The next morning, I told my father what I was doing. He said 'That's all right, Norman will do you a fair deal. Don't forget to have some sort of a guarantee."

"Don't worry Dad, I will be able fix it!" I answered with a grin.

On Sunday morning, John and I met in the Clarence café and had tea and toast. We then walked around to Norman's garage, where the car was parked outside the showroom. It looked very shiny, two toned, black and dark green. I looked at the register plate, it was BDE 58.

We sat inside, it was rather small with two small bucket seats in the front and a small bench seat in the back which was only suitable for two small people. It had no boot and the spare wheel was bolted on the back under the rear window. It was in good condition, as it must have been 'laid up' during the war years.

Then a voice whispered in through the window.

"Interested, Brian? It's for sale." It was Norman, who came from across the road from his home, Weighbridge House, which stood opposite. He was a small gentle man with a mass of fair wavy hair.

"Well maybe. John told me about it last night. What are you asking for it? And don't forget, I'll buy all my petrol from you, if I buy it!" I said with a grin as I got out of the car.

"Well, I want forty notes. It's a good car. And I'll give you three months guarantee, parts and labour".

With that I walked around the car, thinking.

"Sorry Norm. I'll give you thirty five pounds, that's all I've got."

"Well, I'll tell you what, I'll meet you halfway. Thirty-seven and half. That's the best I can do."

I looked across at John. He just smiled and just nodded, as if to say 'take it'.

"Ok, deal done, I think I can just about afford it," I said smiling, as I held my hand out to shake hands with him.

The next evening I paid Norman for the car and Reece collected it and kept it at his garage at Penygarn. I could drive as such, as the guys in work were helpful, showing me hints when I went with them testing vehicles, and Dad took me out several times in the Morris, but I needed some lessons from a professional instructor.

I had several lessons from a man called Frankie Taylor of the Pontypool School of Motoring. He was a shifty looking man with greased down hair.

He arranged for my test on the 5th of August, which was the day before my 18th birthday.

The test centre I had to attend was based at Abergavenny. We went in Frankie's very basic light green Ford Popular. I had a lesson before going around the test course. He told me that there were two examiners, one was a very nice, quiet and a fair examiner, while the other was a six foot four, ex-RAF instructor, with a big black moustache called the Major who was strict and very hard to please and never usually passed anyone first time.

I sat in a waiting room with another youth, about my age from Monmouth, waiting for the examiners to arrive. He sat there gazing around and seemed dim-witted and docile, telling me his mother had been teaching him to drive. He thought it funny when he told me they had scraped their car several times while she was teaching him. The door then opened and out came an examiner, with a clipboard in his hand. He spoke quietly.

"Perkins. Graham Perkins."

"Yes, that's I," the boy answered in broad accent, as he handed him his appointment papers.

"Right, follow me please," said the examiner, as he walked out of the room.

I looked out of the window. They both went to his vehicle, parked on the road, a cream Ford Consul. A smart modern car, covered with a dents and scratches.

Then a cold shudder went through me. I must have the Major, I thought, just my luck.

The door opened and in strode a tall man wearing a thick brown tweed jacket with a clipboard under his arm.

"Jenkins, is it?" he said loudly.

"Yes sir, that's me. Brian Jenkins." I handed him my appointment and he glanced over the form.

"Good, seems everything's in order. Follow me."

I felt tense as he strode outside and then stood by the Ford Popular, glancing at the other examiner getting into the other applicant's larger Ford Consul.

He asked me to read a registration plate on a car across the road to test my eyesight. I read it out.

He just answered with a firm "Correct."

We sat inside and he made himself as comfortable as possible with his clipboard in his hand as it was so cramped for such a tall man. I thought I bet he wished he had the big Ford Consul to go out in. He gave me various instructions and then I drove off.

I began to get more anxious, the weather was getting warm, and I started sweating because I stupidly wore a thick maroon sweater that day.

He then spoke to me in a pleasant tone and asked me would I mind parking on the side while he took of his jacket and that it would be a good idea if I took off my sweater.

I quickly removed it and he made me feel a bit more relaxed.

We carried on with him being very observant, and not saying anything, but writing on his clipboard. We came down a quiet road on the outskirts of Abergavenny, and to our amazement, we followed behind the other learner's car, going slowly with its two nearside wheels on the pavement.

The Major broke his silence and spoke firmly. "Drive around him please."

I looked in my mirror, and drove passed. As we overtook, the Major glanced back.

"What an idiot. People do not realise what we have to put up with. He's on the pavement."

I smiled and said "You're right; it must a worrying time for you?"

"Certainly," he answered abruptly.

I carried on with the test feeling much more confident. After about half an hour and coming to the end of the test, we turned into a small street, near the test centre. There to the left, the Ford Consul was parked on a wide pavement. I drove slowly past them.

The Major turned around inquisitively and I discretely glanced across. In front of the car stood the examiner and the learner, looking at the slightly damaged front grill of the car pressed firmly against a cast iron postbox that stood in front of it.

It was obvious that he must have left the road and hit the postbox. I pulled around the corner and parked in front of the test centre building.

"I'm glad I never had him this morning," the Major said chuckling, as he pondered over his clipboard.

I sat there smiling, thinking about what had happened to the other learner, not thinking about if I'd passed or not.

He then asked me a few questions on the Highway Code.

"Yes, you've done very well, Mr Jenkins. I am going to pass you, but be careful." Then still smiling said "I don't think the other learner passed, do you?"

"I don't think so either, sir!" I answered, feeling very pleased with myself.

That evening, John and I went up to Reece's garage and took of the learner plates. I felt so proud. I decided to drive out to our Aunty Iris and her husband, Derek Hawkins at their home in the countryside between Pontypool and Abergavenny.

My beloved 1938 Morris 8. Cost £37 - 10 shillings

The next day, I proudly drove to work and when I arrived all the staff cheered me and clapped. What a wonderful 18th birthday; it was one of my proudest moments.

That evening after work, as it was my birthday and proud to show off my driving, I squeezed Mam, Dad, Derek and Susan into the car and took them out to a public house near Usk, called the Hall Inn. It was a lovely warm evening and we sat outside and had a meal together. It was a pretty rare moment.

John and I had great times together in that old Morris car, going different places and visiting Aunty Marge and Aunty Gwyn, who by now had married and moved near to Aunty Marge in Newcastle.

We also travelled to Dover and went over to Brussels on the Ferry to see the 1958 World Fair.

September 1958, John and I started the three-year course at the Technical College of Monmouthshire, Crumlin. The class times were one day a week and one evening. Mostly it was theory work, equations, calculations, mathematics and geometry

The class started with about twenty boys, most of them had recently left school, aged about 15 to 16 years old. Some were doing the year again as they had failed their first. You had to pass your first year to enable you to go into the second, then pass the second to enable you to sit the final exam after three years. There were two final grades at the end, a first-class or second-class diploma in motor vehicle mechanics.

I became obsessed trying to do the best I possibly could as I knew if I did not obtain good results after three years, I had nothing to show for my efforts.

All the other boys were indentured mechanics and they did not really have to pass any exams to prove they served their time.

October came, Pam the office girl had gone to another job and was replaced by a dark haired sultry looking girl from Cwmbran, called Penny, who had only recently came to live in the area with her parents. She was about twenty one, three years older than me.

We became good friends and I started to take her out in the car in the evenings and show her the nearby countryside. We went to the cinema and to the Queens Dance hall where we would enjoy ourselves dancing to the Rock and Roll music. We didn't tell any one in work that we were seeing one another.

Late one evening, we parked the car under a disused grandstand at the Polo grounds in New Inn near where we both worked to have a chat about going away somewhere the following weekend.

We began to get passionate towards one another, but the car was so small it was virtually impossible for anything to happen. Therefore, I thought that if I removed the passenger seat as it was only nailed to the wooden floor, and put the seat outside the car, then maybe something might be possible.

I suggested this to Penny, then amid tears of laughter, she said "I've never made love in a car so small, but as you have come up with such a brilliant idea, why not?"

I then forced the seat up from the floor and placed it on the ground outside the car.

Although it was only a fumble in the dark and there was still only a small amount of room in the car, that night Penny took my innocence away from me.

I then placed the seat temporarily back in the car.

Driving home was hilarious as Penny had to hold on to the metal dashboard with both hands, as her seat kept shaking about and flying backward and forward whenever I braked.

The following day at dinner break, I went outside to the car and start nailing the base of seat back in position, while Penny would be laughing from the upstairs office window, saying "don't make it too secure!"

Some of the men begin to wonder what was going on but we never said we were seeing one another.

This occurred a few times until she had to move away with her parents unexpectedly. It was just as well as I would have had to have a new floor in my car sooner than later.

Christmas 1958 and the half term results came through the post from the college with my results showing good promise, but unfortunately, John's was not so good. I said that both of us must keep doing our best.

January came, John started courting a girl named Yvonne, and I didn't see so much of him as usual. However, we still went out to the local dance on Saturday nights.

Susan and Derek were now 7 and 9 years old and attending Pontymoel School.

My Morris car was serving me well, and sometimes I let Dad borrow it to take the family out for a run. I always kept that car in immaculate condition.

I still loved to play my record player and buy the latest records. However, sad news came; the pop world was shocked to hear that on February 3rd 1959, Buddy Holly aged 22, Jiles Richardson, known as the Big Bopper, aged 28, along with 17 years old Ritchie Valens had died in a light aeroplane crash in Iowa.

Holly had seven hit records including a number one in the US and UK with 'That'll be the Day.'

Chapter 17

Saint Valentine's Day

Saturday February 14th, Saint Valentine's Day 1959 and I arrange to meet John in Aldo Bragazes' café on the Clarence to go to the dance at the Queens Ballroom, Pontypool. But he never arrived. I sat there in my dark charcoal suit, white shirt and yellow tie, drinking coffee, wondering why he had not turned up. I assumed that he and his girlfriend had gone somewhere else. I felt rather lonely as it was the first time I had been on my own on a Saturday night.

Aldo stood behind his counter and spoke in his Italian sounding voice.

"You on your own tonight, Squeegee? Where's John?" He always called me that name, I don't know why.

"Yes Aldo, our John hasn't turned up."

"Think he must be in love then."

"I think so too, Aldo."

"Go to the dance on your own, Squeegee. It is special tonight, Saint Valentine's night. You sure to meet somebody."

I will go on my own, I thought, as I knew plenty of boys there to talk to and girls to dance with.

"I'm off, Aldo. I think I'll go to the dance."

"Well done, Squeegee. Have a good time."

I collected my car from around the corner, drove into town and parked at the top of the market, and into the Dance hall I strode.

After about two hours chatting to Tony Morgan and Mike Taylor and dancing with several girls, I noticed a small quiet girl stood on the side with her friends. She looked ever so sweet and pleasant.

"Can I have a dance with you please? I can't dance all that good, but it's only a slow foxtrot," I said shrugging my shoulders and holding my hands out.

She glanced at her friends who looked on approvingly, and came towards me.

"I'm not that good myself," she answered with a pleasant smile.

"I haven't seen you here before," I said as we started dancing.

"No," she replied, "I've only just started coming here lately with my friends. Do you come here often?"

"Yes, I've been coming here about a year now. I think maybe I'm a few years older than you - I'm eighteen," I answered.

"Oh, I'm only fifteen. Sixteen in two weeks time."

We started chatting away and after several dances, I became aware that I seemed so relaxed in her company.

"What's your name, if you don't mind me asking?"

"It's Dianne. Dianne Kendall."

"Pleased to meet you, Dianne. I'm Brian Jenkins."

"Nice to meet you. Do you come here often on your own, Brian?"

"No, this is the first time. I was supposed to meet with my cousin, John Rowland, but I think he's gone out with his new girlfriend."

She then introduced me to her friends and as the evening passed by, we had a few cups of tea together. She told me that she lived in Newman Road, Trevethin, a housing estate above Pontypool with her mother and father and that she had a younger sister, Jane and an older brother, Desmond.

"I know your Des," I said surprised. "He used to go to Abersychan Tec School where I went to."

As it was nearly time to go home, I asked hopefully "do you mind if I take you home? I've got a car. It's parked at the back of the market."

"A car? You have a car?" she answered surprised.

"Yes, but it's only a Morris 8."

"I don't know much about cars, but you're lucky."

"Suppose I am really, but I've been working before I left school and ever since."

"Where do you live? Have you got very far to go home?"

"No, I live near Clarence Street, not far," I answered, hoping she wouldn't ask which part. I was aware that the area I lived was still frowned upon.

She looked over to her friends, who sat nearby, for a kind of approval.

"Do you mind girls if I go home with Brian?"

They all said it was all right as long as I got her home safe. I drove her home and kissed her goodnight. I felt so pleased to have met her and arranged to see her the next morning as it was a Sunday.

We continued seeing each other and going out regularly to the cinema and dances. I liked her parents and adored her sister Jane, who was only about thirteen years old. Her mother's name was Olwyn, but I always called her 'Mother'. Her father Roy, who I always called Mr Kendall, was a very firm strict person. I always had to bring her home by half past ten unless it was a special occasion. I was always very respectful of him and feared him slightly, although I guess tt never did me any harm.

I was always welcomed to their home as one of the family and when I came home from college late in the evening, there was always a special meal prepared for me. We spent many good times together in the company of Dianne's married cousin Ann and her husband Derek Spanswich, going out on Saturday nights and weekend trips to London.

With Susan in 1960 outside our new council house, Trevethin

July came and it was time for the college class to sit the first year exam of our City and Guilds. It seemed so vital that I pass, I had done as much studying as I possibly could have.

John and I travelled over to the college armed with our studying and Logarithm books, reading as much as we could before the exam. As I sat at my desk and looked at the exam papers I felt so helpless without any books for me to refer to.

After the exam we left the room and I went outside feeling exhausted. I spoke to John. "It was quite hard, wasn't it but I think I managed most of the questions."

I was rather surprised when he answered back and said "I rather thought it was easy." This worried me slightly, as I thought it was difficult.

A few pensive weeks followed then a report arrived from the college through the post, with the first year's results.

I opened the envelope and scanned the page. It had printed a list of all the names in the class that had sat the exam with a percentage of pass next to each name.

A red line printed across the page divided the names of the pupils. The ones with 50 percent or higher were above the line and had passed; the ones under the line with less than 50 percent had failed.

I franticly looked at the names below and was overjoyed for a moment that I wasn't among them. Then I saw the name John Rowland below the line. I was gutted, John had failed. I felt dreadful. I then started to read up the page. A few Pontypool boys appeared, Malcolm Hodge, Ken Lewis and Alan Phillips. They had passed as well.

I then looked higher up the list and realised my name was on top of with a 85 percent pass. I couldn't believe it, all my efforts had turned out so well.

My joy was tinged with disappointment as I began to realise John would not be coming with me next year and wished for a moment that I had never started the course.

John never returned to the college and later finished working for Norman Jenkins and went to work for a milk delivery firm.

The next day, I took the results into work and went upstairs and handed it to Mr Gilbert when he arrived. He read the result and looked very pleased with himself, saying he would send the result to Colonel Pye.

I then told all the mechanics at tea break of my result. They were also pleased for me. I later received a letter from the M D, complimenting me on my early success and hoping I would continue with my progress.

My life was still being overshadowed with bad dreams and my mother and father's relationship. Dad was beginning to drink too much as it was easy for him to call in a public house on his grocery rounds. Still living down Mill Road didn't help, with the tip now only yards away from the road in front of our house and Mam complaining all the time to Dad about the conditions we lived in.

October 1959 and they received a letter from the council with the fantastic news that they were allocated a new three bed roomed council house at Belle Vue Close, Trevethin. It was the best news they had had since they got married 19 years ago.

I felt so good on hearing the news, no more being embarrassed to say where I lived, and no more living in between a refuse tip and a dirty gasworks that showered us with coal dust and smoke.

The day we moved was full of excitement. It had three bedrooms; Mam and Dad had one, Susan had her own room, while Derek and I shared the other.

It was a longer distance for me to travel to work, but it was well worth it, if only by having a decent room to eat in and by being able to bath when I got home without boiling pans of water and sitting in a tin bath.

Susan was now eight and Derek ten and they changed schools to one nearby called Snatch Wood.

About this time, I decided to sell my Morris 8 car and I bought a 1954 Black Hillman Minx. As it had a much worn engine, I bought it very cheap and later fitted a new engine myself.

It was a smart looking car with modern looks, a column gear change and plenty of room for five people. It had an unusual number plate, 1Y 7117.

My 1954 Hillman Minx

1960 heralded in new decade called the swinging sixties with rock and roll at its peak. I was still making good practical progress both as a trainee mechanic and with the theory course at the college.

I was seeing Dianne regularly, going to dances everywhere and still having a late meal at her house after college. We enjoyed visiting her grandmother

Sara Jane. For some reason, they all called her 'Nar'. She was a lovely old lady, I liked her so much.

During the warm summer, a Royal wedding took place at Westminster Abbey on the 6th of May, between Princess Margaret, the Queens sister, and Anthony Armstrong Jones. More than 20 million viewers tuned in to watch the first ever televised Royal wedding.

Sad news blighted Wales the next month. In June, 45 miners had been killed in a coal mine explosion at nearby Six Bells colliery. It started from a build up of coal gas, ignited by a spark from a falling stone. It was, again, sad news to hear of so many miners losing their lives, as many had done in the past.

August 1960 and my results arrived from the end of the second year at college. I had achieved top marks again and passed, along with the eight other boys left in the class, to gain entrance to the final year.

That autumn for some reason I decided to stop seeing Dianne and spend more time out by myself and seeing other friends. As the weeks went by, I began to miss her terribly and just ached to see her. Life felt so aimless.

My heart pounded every time I drove past her house. But my pride for some reason couldn't bring me to ask to her to be back together again. My college work didn't mean much to me and it seemed that I had nothing to live for. Then I began to realise that I loved her and wanted to be with her always, but feared I might lose her.

I came home one evening from college feeling very low. I made up my mind to go over to her house and ask to see her. I was ready to go, when the back door opened. With my mind in a haze, I couldn't believe it. There stood Dianne. She had thought the same way. I put my arm around her and tears followed. We then both realised we were both more than just fond of one another.

Later that year at the work's Christmas dinner party, I asked her to marry me and we became engaged on March 2nd 1961, Dianne's eighteenth birthday.

Senator John Kennedy was sworn in as President of the United States on January the 20th and in April came the world shattering news that Russia had successfully launched the first man into space, Yuri Gagarin. This was followed in May by the first American in space, Alan Shepard.

Later that summer, I studied hard for the final City and Guilds year and with my 21st birthday getting near and my training at work coming to an end, it was essential I got a good result in the examination in July, with the results due early August.

With Dianne in a photo booth 1959

On August 9th came news that an airline passenger plane carrying teachers and pupils from Lanfranc school in Croydon near London had crashed between two mountains' when trying to land at Sola Airport, Stavanger in Norway. Mam was worried and concerned because my cousin Peter, Aunty Olwyn's son, attended that school. Sadly hours later, it was confirmed that Peter, aged 14 was one of over a hundred passengers and crew killed in the accident.

It was a terrible shock to all the family and my mother, along with many of her brothers and sisters from all over the country attended the funeral in Croyden.

Following my July exams, I waited for the postman early every morning. Then on the 4th August, a brown envelope arrived in the post from City and Guilds, London. My hand trembled as I opened it and slowly read the words. I had obtained a first class pass with honours. I was absolutely overjoyed. Mam, Dad, Derek and Susan looked on as tears flowed down my cheeks. I immediately went over to Dianne's house to inform her of the good news. I was so proud to go to work that day and show the results to the manager and work mates and later that week, I received a letter from the Managing Director congratulating me and amending my salary to full vehicle technician.

It was a wonderful 21st birthday for me. I had finally made something of my life after three years of trying and remembering the past, skin diseased hands from the flour and the times on the railway, and leaving school with no qualifications.

Dianne and I decided to get married in the August of 1962. We started saving together. Firstly, we were going to buy a new house but everyone said 'Don't put a noose around your neck,' so I decided against it, a decision I always regretted. I sold the Hillman car for a hundred pounds and used it as a deposit against a small terraced house, which cost five hundred pounds; the remainder was put on a private mortgage with the owner from Cardiff.

The house was in the middle of a terrace called Lower Bridge Street, just of the other side of the Clarence which Michael and I used to pass on our way to Park Terrace school. We both started to make the house habitable, as it had been empty for a long period but it was difficult doing it on our own, as neither of us knew anything about building work. It was a big mistake buying that house. We had plenty of enthusiasm, but not much practical building knowledge and not aware of the difficulty of renovating an old house, I couldn't see behind the crumbling plaster work and old latch doors and flagstone floors. I should have had more sense and learned from what I knew about old houses, from living down Mill Road. After so much work, and the house using up both our wages, it became difficult to find the money to complete it on time.

We decided to still get married in the August and stay with Dianne's parents after our honeymoon, until we finished the house.

We got married on the 18th of August 1962 at Saint Luke's church, Pontnewynydd, about one mile north of Pontypool and had the reception at a Dance club in Pontypool. Derek Spanswick was Best Man. Susan, Jane and Dianne's cousins Gillian, Gaynor and Linda were bridesmaids. My cousin David Beer and Dianne's cousin Robert Bond were ushers.

Our wedding day, August 18th 1962

As I didn't have a car, Aunty Iris kindly loaned us their cream Morris Minor to go touring with on our Honeymoon.

Before we left, Dianne left her bouquet of yellow roses on the grave of her father's brother, Cliff, who had died recently after a long illness.

We drove to Newquay in Cornwall, then drove across the South Coast, stopping at Torquay, Fareham and Brighton then going up to London and staying at Aunty Mill's house at Teddington for a few days. She and Uncle Jim made us very welcome and we enjoyed the company of cousin David and his girlfriend Carol and went out with then on several occasions.

We returned from our honeymoon with no money and stayed at Dianne's parents until we made our house livable, thanks to the help of Dianne's mother and her grandmother, 'Nar', helping paper the walls. We moved in about two months later, but still had no bathroom.

1963 came and life became difficult as money was very short with trying to furnish the home, and finding out that Dianne was expecting a baby in June.

At work, two new men had started work with us. I was pleased because one was the same age as me. His name was Rhys Reese. He had just got married and had a new baby son named Dale. He came from a place called Pantegasseg, where Uncle Ted done his grocery rounds. The other was fitter's mate Hayward Teague.

Rhys and I became good work mates together. I used to teach him all about the theory part of mechanics. We had many good laughs, cheering one another up during our difficult times.

On June the 2nd, I took Dianne into Cefn Ila Nursing Home near Usk. The next day we had a son and named him Martyn Anthony.

Not having a car at the time, Rhys loaned me his little powder blue van to collect them both from the nursing home to bring them home. Ironically, Dianne wore a powder blue dress that day and looked as smart as she always did.

I found the next few years were the most difficult time of our lives. I don't know if I cannot, or do not want to remember them, with the house still wanting a lot of work and Dianne finishing her job at the Nylon Factory, things became more difficult.

Martyn arrived ten months after we got married, much earlier than we had anticipated, both of us being so naïve at the time. We were so anxious for some extra money that I took a part time job in the evenings at the Clarence Hotel as a barman. I would hurry home from work and change into a white shirt and black dickybow tie and serve drinks from behind the bar in the lounge until they closed.

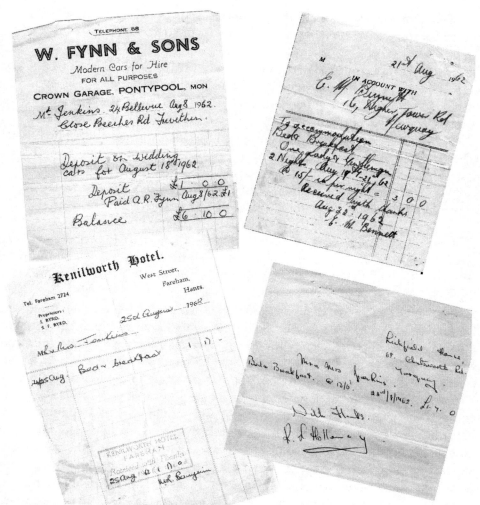

Wedding day car hire receipt and bed and breakfast receipts at Torquay, Newquay and Fareham while on honeymoon

On the 22nd of November 1963, the dreadful news came that evening that President Kennedy was dead after being shot during a motor cavalcade with the governor of Dallas in Texas. It made an uneasy tension throughout the world

The next month brought sad family news that Uncle Alf, Mam's brother, had been knocked down by a train while working on the railway track near the village of Goytre and had died from his injuries. He was the first one of the 15 brothers and sisters to die and sadly from an accident.

7th of February 1964 saw Beatle mania arrive in America. The four members of the British hit band arrived in New York to start their first tour of the United States. Everywhere the excitement over the Beatles' arrival reached almost fever pitch.

On the 25th of February, Dianne and I stayed up late to watch Cassius Clay Win the heavyweight champion of the world, after beating Sony Liston in one of the biggest upset in boxing History.

October this year saw Harold Wilson narrowly wining the general election to put Labour into power after 13 years of Conservative government.

After about three years of marriage, things began to improve and I had saved enough money to have a new bath suite fitted into a small bedroom. I was also able to buy a small Austin van, to which I fitted seats and side windows into the rear.

Our lives began to improve and I was able to spend more time with Dianne and Martyn. We started going out to the countryside in the van with Dianne's mam and dad. They began to enjoy the pleasure of their grandson, which brought us all closer together. Jane had a new boyfriend, a guy named Cedric Haycock from Newport and she was planning to get married soon.

But unfortunately this new found happy period came to a suddenly abrupt end. One evening in February 1966, we visited Dianne's parents with Martyn. I started chatting to her father in the living room when he unexpectedly seemed very unwell. They sent for a doctor, who after diagnosing him, stated that Mr Kendall had suffered a mild heart attack and, as a precaution, sent for an ambulance to take him to hospital. Before he went, Mr Kendall insisted he changed and cleaned his shoes. He was a very particular person and walked smartly out of the house. I took Mr Kendall to the hospital while Dianne stayed at the house with Jane and our Martyn.

A few hours later, I brought Mrs Kendall back to her home and we stayed the night with her and Jane. I left early in the morning to go to work. A few hours later, I phoned the hospital and was taken back to hear he had passed away during the night. I immediately left work and returned to their house.

The family was shattered, he was only 52 years old. Dianne was only 22 and Jane only 20. We contacted Desmond who was living away from home and gave him the sad news.

That weekend after the funeral, I felt a sense of maturity, with a responsibility and loyalty towards Dianne and her family. A few months later, Jane married Cedric Haycock in Pontypool and went to live in Newport.

July 30th 1966 and England won the World Cup against West Germany at Wembley. About 400 million people around the world watched the televised match. Even the Welsh and the Scots rejoiced at their triumph that summer.

Autumn came and the evening of October the 21st will live in my memory forever. Jane and Cedric had made arrangements to visit us for the evening but early that day more 130 people, mainly children had had been killed by a coal slag tip overlooking the welsh village of Aberfan near Merthyr Tydfil. At least over 100 children had been confirmed dead after the tip had engulfed the school at 9.15 that morning. Instead of pleasant evening together, we watched on the television the awful scenes of a rescue bid of about 200 men under floodlight searching for any survivors and pulling out the dead. The final death toll was 144 lives lost.

Since leaving my parents home to get married, their relationship seemed to have worsened though drink. Dad had given up his greengrocery round and tried to manage a small greengrocery shop at Trevethin with my mother. But this didn't work out and my father had to finally give up selling greengrocery after more than 25 years.

Dad managed to obtain a manual job working in a local factory in Cwmbran, but was still drinking whenever he could. My mother was no help to him; she thought more about playing bingo every night instead of giving him the love and comfort he deserved.

Better times came in 1967, as I began to pay off any dept I owed from furnishing and improving the home and was able to buy a three year old Ford Cortina car, which was a big improvement over my Austin van.

Mam and Dad had changed their council house for one near Cwmbran to enable Dad to get to work easier.

We had previously decided to enlarge the family and on the 2nd of July 1967, again at Cefn Ila nursing home, Dianne gave birth to another son, Richard John.

Ten days later on the 12th July, Martyn and Richard had their first cousin.

Jane presented Cedric with the arrival of their first baby, a boy. They named him Andrew.

It was the end of 1967 and I received a letter from the solicitors that my private mortgage with the owner had ended and that I could collect the deeds from their office.

This was great news. After five years of struggle to pay and renovate, the Bridge Street house was finally paid for. A few weeks later a three bedroomed house appeared for sale on the Broadway, Pontypool.

'The Broadway' was good area to live. It was a long sweeping road with Victorian bay-fronted houses with gardens in front, overlooking Pontypool with a good view over the park and rugby ground.

I enquired about the price and it was £2800. We both viewed it. It was empty at the time and needed completely re-decorating, but we both liked it and decided to buy it. I managed to sell our own house for £1000. I then used £500 as a deposit and the remainder on fitting central heating, re-decorating and carpeting the whole house before we moved in, as we were fortunate to be able to have the keys early before completion.

We moved into 58, The Broadway in the January of 1968. I felt like a king as I looked out over at the beautiful crisp winter view of Pontypool Park and the distant village of New Inn.

That evening, I felt proud and happy as we tucked Richard snugly into his cot and put Martyn into his own lovely warm bedroom. What a difference in five years, since the early cold struggle days of Bridge Street. Martyn started school at Wainfelin Infant school nearby with several of his friends. The following years on the Broadway were happy ones, except for the fact my father would come and visit and tell me how unhappy he was, but I believed if he'd had more thought and love for his grandchildren, he would have been a more content person rather than seeking love from my mother.

Christmas 1968 came and we witnessed the American Apollo Eight Space Mission to the moon, which enabled three American astronauts to leave earth and circle the moon several times and return. This was the first time any human being was able to view the earth from 250,000 miles away and witness an earthrise instead of a sunrise. After following the space race since it began, I became exited because on the 16th of July 1969, the Apollo 11 mission blasted from Cape Kennedy. The hopes of the world were with them for being the first ever human beings to land on the moon's surface. Days later on the evening of the 21st, I stayed up all night and saw on television live pictures of the spacecraft Eagle land on the surface of the moon. Later I saw Neil Armstrong emerge from the craft and walk on the surface followed twenty minutes later by Buzz Aldrin. The historic event was enabled to be televised by cameras installed aboard Eagle and turned on by Armstrong.

Times were good, going on holidays to Devon and Cornwall with Jane, Cedric and Andrew. Susan had been courting a boy named Wayne Preston for a long time and they seemed well suited together. They became engaged on the 28th of March 1970.

My job at Co-ordinated Contracts was beginning to make me feel unhappy. I had been there since I was seventeen and many new faces appeared that I felt I was part of the furniture. A new company had come to the area called Crane Fruehauf Trailers, just up the road from us. They were advertising for mechanics, so I went along and spoke to the Manager who said I could start there whenever I wanted to.

I started working at Crane's Fruehauf in the spring of 1970, but still stayed very friendly with the men from Co-ordinated and was always grateful to the opportunity they gave me.

I had only been as at Crane's for a few months and began to learn an added skill, electric welding. I teamed up with a fellow worker much younger than me, Alex Edwards. We became great friends and had a great working relationship. I worked there for about six months until the manager made me the workshop foreman.

Summer came and surprise, surprise, Jane and Dianne were both expecting new arrivals. On the 18th of December Jane gave birth to another boy and named him Steven, while Dianne had to wait until February the 12th to present me with yet another boy who we called Jonathan James. It seemed to be all boys now.

While Dianne was in the nursing home, the country changed over to decimal currency on the 14th of February 1971, Saint Valentines Day. Later in the year, on the 21st of August, Susan married Wayne at St Michael's church, Llanvehangle and in September, Richard started school joining Martyn at Wainfelin Infant school.

I became disillusioned working at Crane Fruehauf mainly because of dishonest management. The works and stores managers went out drinking in the afternoon with office girls and not organising the place properly. Being the workshop foreman, I felt under unnecessary pressure. As a result, I read the local Argus for a change of job, and found a company named Willowdean

Garages in Newport, advertising for mechanics with a much better rate of pay. I called there and the owner Mr Parish said I could start whenever I liked. So I gave notice to Crane Fruehauf and started working in Newport. The travelling was a bit of a bind, but at least I was a lot happier.

Some days I would call in to Cwmbran to visit my parents as it was on the way from Newport. Dad was still drinking regularly. They surprised me by saying my brother Derek was making their life a misery whenever he came home, as he was always going away to some college or working away somewhere, but my visits never seemed to resolve anything.

Our next door neighbour on The Broadway happened to be Bill Vinycombe, who used to manage the Fagots and Peas café at the top of the market in Pontypool. He was still a jolly looking man and a keen member of the Salvation Army. We got very friendly together, chatting about old times. He was now retired, but sadly his wife had died several years before.

He had difficulty in walking, but one day later in the year, he was just able to manage to walk to the rear of our house to show me a car of his that, unknown to me, had been stored in his garage for about eight years, since his wife had died.

It was a black 1962 Austin Cambridge, with very little mileage on the clock. It looked a sad sight covered in thick dust with all tyres flat and perished.

I checked the car over and found the brakes and engine was seized and unusable.

"Would you like to buy it at a reasonable price, Brian?" he said to me in a sad tone. "I would love to see it parked down on the front road like it used to be, when my wife used to sit in it."

"I don't really want to, Bill. It will take a lot of work, and a lot of time. It's not my type of car, but I'll have a word with Dianne and let you know."

After a few days thought, I decided to buy the car and bring it back it its original condition. This took me several months, working on it in the evenings in my garage, stripping down the engine and brakes and bringing the body work back to a good condition.

When I had finally finished the car, I drove it around and parked it in front of Mr Vinecombe's house.

He got up out of his chair and looked through the window. Tears came to his eyes as he looked at the shiny black car parked on the road in front of his house.

"Thank you, Brian. You've made a dream come true for me. I can imagine my dear wife sat in that car as she so often did in the past."

I kept the car until Bill sadly died years later. We drove to the burial ground behind the funeral car in that lovely old Cambridge.

I enjoyed working at Willowdean Garages. There was about eight other mechanics working there. I grew to like Newport, everything seemed so busy there as it was a very large town with plenty of traffic and seemed full of life.

Chapter 18

The sun always seems to shine in New Inn

One Saturday morning in May 1972 while working at Willowdean, John Crowley, the workshop manager came to tell me that someone had an important message for me on the phone in the office. It was my mother's next door neighbour. She informed me that Dad had been taken to the Royal Gwent hospital in Newport in an ambulance accompanied with my mother, as he seemed unconscious and she was unable to arouse him that morning.

I removed my overhauls and immediately drove over to the hospital and where I found Dad in the emergency department led on a trolley. He was breathing and the staff were trying to diagnose his unconsciousness. My mother was in a nearby waiting room sat on a chair.

"What do you think is the matter with him?" I asked the doctor.

He replied "I don't know yet, but I suspect tablets. We've asked Mrs Jenkins and all she knows is he went out for drink. He was in bed when she came home, but failed to revive him this morning. He should be sober by now, that's if he was drunk going to bed."

I shuddered to think what might have happened as I held my father's hand and spoke to him, with no reply, only heavy breathing. I turned to my mother and said "I don't think Dad has been taking any tablets lately, has he, Mam?"

"No, because I always collect everything from the chemist," she replied.

With that the doctor spoke.

"I must send him to the intensive care unit upstairs immediately to deal with him. His stomach may be pumped as a precaution."

"I want to go with him," I replied. My mother stayed down in the outpatient's waiting room.

I walked alongside the trolley with the men who were taking Dad upstairs. My mind turned over about what could have happened.

When we came to the doors of the intensive care ward, a woman doctor stopped me and asked who I was. I explained he was my father.

"Mr Jenkins, we will keep you informed," she said as she showed me to a small room with two old armchairs inside. "I think you should wait in this room for the time being. Would you like a cup of tea brought to you?"

"No thanks," I answered, gratefully.

I glanced back at my father, still breathing heavy as he entered the unit. Under my breath, I was saying "please Dad, don't die and leave me as there is so much I want to do for you."

I waited a few seconds then entered the room and closed the large old Victorian door behind me. I looked around the small room that needed decorating badly with wallpaper hanging loose. I sat down and looked out of the window at the view of Newport with the docks in the distance. It was a lovely sunny morning. Dianne and I had planned to take the boys to Rest Bay in Porthcawl, as we often visited the coast on Saturday afternoons after I finished work.

My mind was in turmoil. All I could picture was my father breathing on that trolley. My mind flashed back to the days in Halifax, during the war years, his days as a miner coming home from the mines, and all the years he went around the roads selling fruit and veg, with me in a little black plastic mackintosh sat behind him on the cart, being pulled by our horse, Jennifer.

My thoughts came to the present and I promised myself that if he came out of that room alright, I would definitely do something to try and sort his life out.

After about twenty minuets, the uncanny silence of that little room was broken, as the large door creaked open and the doctor stood there. I looked across at her, hoping she would say he was alright. She came over to me and put her hand on my shoulder.

"I am sorry to tell you, Mr Jenkins, we done everything we possibly could. I am afraid we lost him, your father has just died."

I immediately got up and walked past her.

"Oh no, he can't have," I said angrily, as I entered the unit, and looked at my father lying still on the trolley. I ran my hand over his sparse grey hair. He was only 55 years old and looked 75.

"What happened to him?"

"His heart just gave out it, could not cope. We think from an overdose of tablets but we will confirm this after a post mortem."

I was devastated to think that only the day before I had waved goodbye to him from their doorstep in the evening, after calling in from work.

I went down to tell my mother what had happened and we walked slowly out to my car in the carpark. The ride home was rather strange and silent. She said she would inform Derek as he was away at the time.

I said I would let Susan know when she arrived home, as she was away on holiday. She should have been home by now but her flight had been delayed. I was thinking it would be a terrible shock to her, as she was only a young girl of twenty, similar to Dianne when she lost her father so young. I then began to get bitter about what had happened as I tried to concentrate on driving my mother back home.

I pulled up outside her front door and suddenly pulled the hand brake on hard. I looked across at Mam as I got out of the car.

"Do you know where he went to last night? Who he was with and where Dad got the tablets from?" I asked angrily. Mam opened her front door and went inside.

"Don't blame me, I don't know where he was. I think he met a man called Peter."

"I'm not blaming you, Mam, but Dad knew where you were and so you should have known where he was," I said, still feeling really angry. "I'm going home now to tell Dianne and Dad's brothers and sisters at Penygarn. I'll call into Wayne's family too in case Susan goes there first from holiday. We will come down later this evening to see you're alright, Mam," I said.

My mother's neighbour came in to keep her company while I drove home, feeling how after all these years of trying to make things good between my parents that it should end this way.

Dad had deserved better than this, but at least he was now at peace with himself.

During the funeral, I was surprised and moved to see how many people from in the past attended, and how he was liked by so many people, even his customers from years before. Richard Jenkins came on behalf of his father Norman Jenkins who had emigrated to Australia.

After the funeral, I felt a huge loss. It was different calling in on my mother without Dad being there.

The post mortem showed Dad had taken an overdose of barbiturate tablets. I traced the person who had given them to Dad, but I never knew whether the overdose of tablets was taken deliberately or by mistake.

The following months throughout the summer of 1972 were good for our family at Broadway, but I felt for change. It seemed we had not many friends, only Jane and Cedric. I visited the workmen's club with John some evenings but it all seemed very humdrum. Even the neighbours around us were elderly and kept to themselves.

As the end of the year approached, good news came with a surprise - the first girl to the family. Susan had given birth to a baby girl named Melissa on the 19th of December.

The early seventies, with prosperity, brought a new era of private urban housing development throughout Wales, and as I looked out of our windows, I could see in the distance this happening in the lower regions of Pontypool, New Inn and Cwmbran.

Days later, we both happened to be looking out over New Inn together and I said to Dianne

"They're building new houses out there in New Inn, I wouldn't mind a new house, and it would be nearer for me to go to work."

She replied, "Not only that, but when we look out over there, it seems the sun always seem to shine over New Inn."

I smiled and answered, "Let's go down there and look at the new houses being built."

We later put the boys in the car and drove down to the site at which they were building. We looked at several houses being built in and around a road called Golf Road leading off the main highway to Newport. Some were completed and seemed good value at £7000.

"We would be able to buy one if we sold our house at Broadway," I said excitedly.

That evening we both sat down and agreed if any houses were still left for sale, it would be a good idea and nice to have a newly built house. It would also be easier for me to go to work in Newport. The boys' education would not be a problem; Martyn could remain at his infant school until his 11 plus in two years time, and Richard had only attended there two years so he could move to the local school at Green Lawn, New Inn.

The next day we visited the estate agents handling the sale of the new homes and were informed that all the plots had been sold except one off Golf Road in a cul -de-sac called Russell Close, because someone had cancelled the purchase the day before.

We drove to New Inn to look at the Russell Close site only to see the bases, no road and everything a quagmire of mud. We inspected the vacant plot and found it very pleasing. It was to have three bedrooms and a garage on the side, with the view looking back up towards Pontypool. We then both agreed a change would be good for us.

We drove back to the estate agents and signed a contract for them to sell our house and buy the available plot. We were informed that it would be about three months before our new house would be ready to move into.

The next few months went by very quickly, and they managed to sell our house early, so no problems emerged.

Some evenings I would call in and view the progress of the house on my way home from work in Newport.

Every day as I travelled to Newport, I passed a tall stack emerging from a chemical works being built at the lower end of New Inn. I was intrigued to know what they were building and so enquired one evening. I was informed by the man in the Weighbridge office that a chemical waste disposal plant called Re Chem. was being built there.

A few days later, two weeks before Christmas, an advertisement appeared in the South Wales Argus newspaper for a qualified heavy goods vehicle mechanic in New Inn. Applicants were to write to Biffa Waste Services Ltd, Re Chem., New Inn, Pontypool.

I became interested as it seemed to be a good idea; I would be living only about half a mile from the site, when we move into our new house.

I wrote in and had an interview for the job, calling in from work one evening. I was interviewed by someone from head office and the new Biffa depot Manager, Nigel Coombs.

They needed a mechanic that would work on his own and help build up a new branch of waste disposal vehicles to an unknown number, subject to the growth of the branch, for which to cover South Wales.

I was shown around a small, but newly built workshop that was completely empty of equipment and stores. It seemed a good opportunity for someone to start at the beginning. I was asked several questions about my experience and my attitude to going along with the company as it expanded. I replied that it was just the opening I wanted.

I was told that five other applicants had to be interviewed, and that I would be informed within a week of the outcome.

A week later, a letter arrived offering me the position and that I could begin at the start of February. Christmas came and over the festive season we prepared to move into the new house. It was such an exciting time, and it gave me time to think about the job offer.

January 1973 and we moved to 4 Russell Close, New Inn, and I wrote and accepted the job with Biff Waste Services.

I started work at the beginning of February. The manager, Nigel Coombs, was installed in his office with a secretary.

Two drivers started, Cliff Harrison and Lyn Strange, followed by Peter James.

I began opening accounts with parts suppliers and ordered equipment for the workshops. I started to build a spare parts stock and prepare vehicle maintenance programs. It was an exiting period as we began to expand the fleet with four tankers to maintain supplied by Re Chem. for the collection of their liquid waste.

Nigel then employed a young salesman, Terry Osmond, who became a brilliant force within our young close team. Business expanded rapidly, thanks to Terry's sales ability and motivation. Many more vehicles were added to the fleet every month, and more drivers employed to drive them.

The move to New Inn opened a new life for us; a new house, new young neighbours, Mostyn and Helen Jones, next door bringing up their families. I joined the local social club, called Green Lawn and met new friends like Wyndom and Joy Evans, Bernard and Francis Humphries, Bunny and Kay Watkins, Garry Meehan and Dennis Tipping, to name a few. We enjoyed evenings out, weekend trips to anywhere and a few 'men only' International rugby trips thrown in as well. Great times with great people.

1974 and Martyn passed his Eleven Plus exams and entered West Mon grammar school in September. We were all very exited and proud on the day, seeing him in his new uniform.

Friends from New Inn in Dartmouth

The next year, Susan gave birth to another girl, Rebecca, on the 17th of July. Dianne started work at the nearby County Hospital as an auxiliary nurse.

Sadly her grandmother, 'Nar' passed away in June 1976.

The following years saw the depot expand enormously with hundreds of waste containers with the Biffa logo painted on them covering all parts of South Wales.

Although it was exciting times watching our depot grow, it was hard work and it became impossible for me to maintain such a growing fleet of vehicles and the hundreds of containers.

After discussions with Nigel, it was agreed that we should start another mechanic and I suggested my past work friend, who was still at Crane Fruehauf, Alex Edwards, a person I knew would give us every support. Although Alex was not an experienced diesel mechanic, I knew my knowledge and supervision would soon pass on to him easily and we could always rely on one another.

We opened a further depot in Port Talbot. Nigel became Area Manager and Terry Osmond deservedly became Sales Manager of South Wales.

Then a routing clerk was employed, followed by tyre fitter John Thorly, another mechanic Sid Jones and welder Andrew Watkins.

I became workshop manager, and was appointed a member of the Institute of Road Transport Engineers.

Biffa workmates, 1980

Biffa now became the biggest waste disposable company in South Wales with about thirty vehicles, and we began to outgrow our premises so the company bought a larger site about a half mile away. It happened to be the same building at New Road, New Inn, as when I started my mechanical training back in 1957 with Co-ordinated Contracts.

September 1978, the thrill this year was to see Richard smartly dressed in his uniform, joining Martyn at West Mon after passing his Eleven Plus.

Jane and Cedric were now holidaying regularly in their caravan, so we decided to buy one as well. All the five boys had great times on holidays together, mostly touring Devon and Cornwall.

The following year, Dianne decided she would start training as a qualified nurse along with our friend Joy Evans. They attended Neville Hall Hospital, Abergavenny for the next three years. It was difficult times for her, with running a home and bringing up our family, and especially with me never knowing when I would be home from work.

My brother Derek got married in February 1980 and was to have five children, Simon, Nicholas, Stuart, Amy and Liam.

Martyn, now 18, started at Cardiff University in 1981 doing a degree in Zoology and the following year Jonathan joined Richard at West Mon School. He looked very smart in the changed colours of West Mon, now a comprehensive school.

1982 and Susan was expecting her third child. On the 28th of May, another girl was born, Lucy Jayne. But sadly little Lucy was born with Spina Bifida and it came as a severe traumatic shock to the family. All our hearts felt full of sorrow for them in their distress.

Dianne's nursing skills was exceptionally supportive towards them in their time of anguish. About six weeks later, we took Melissa and Rebecca along with Jonathan for a week's holiday, and while we were away, Lucy passed away. It was a very heartbreaking time for Susan and Wayne to lose someone they dearly cared for.

Later, Dianne, along with Joy, completed her training at Abergavenny. Our whole family was very proud of her as she passed to become a state-enrolled nurse. A great achievement being a wife and mother of three boys.

Dianne then started her new career in the stroke unit at the County Hospital, Panteg near Pontypool. Richard also left school this year to become an Apprentice in Engineering.

Photograph of Uncle Reese and cousin John Rowland in 1975

We had great times with the caravan, but in 1983 Dianne, Cedric, Jane and I decided to go on a camping holiday with the five boys near Beziers in the south of France, with a company called Gwent Camping, run by a man called John Price. The company would organise a coachload of people, mainly school teachers and pupils, and would travel down every fortnight. The coach would then return to Britain with the previous fortnight's campers. A person was employed and stationed there permanently to oversee the arrival of new campers, make sure they 'settled in' and to sort out any problems that might occur. This person was nicknamed the 'camp commandant'.

By coincidence, when we joined the bus to France, two old school friends were sat in front of us. It was Mike Taylor, with his partner Pauline, the same Mike Taylor that used to work for Norman Jenkins in the late fifties.

We all had a very good time together in France and we remained friends with them when we returned home, going out together regularly.

We became good friends with Mike's parents, Frank and Iris and his two brothers, Brian and Garry.

In the summer of 1983, Dianne's brother, Desmond and his partner, who were now living in Hull, came home to visit us and their mother for a few days. It was good to see Des after he had been away for several years.

Sadly in the late autumn of 1984, Desmond returned home to Wales, gravely ill and stayed with us for a short time until he passed away at Home Towers, Penarth on the 23rd of December, aged 43.

May 1985 saw our first holiday abroad without the children. Mike and Pauline invited us to go with them to visit the Greek island of Zante for two weeks. It was one the most exiting and enjoyable holiday we ever had.

With wet weekends and the boys being teenagers, understandably they started to moan about coming with us in the caravan. So we decided to take an offer made to us from John Price of Gwent Tenting to lease a plot of ground at his camp in France where I could site our caravan permanently. Jane and Cedric agreed to share the cost, and we towed the van down together to the south of France in February 1986.

A few months later, Mike and Pauline had parted, and Mike returned to live with his parents. He was now out of work and at a crossroads with his life.

The windows and guttering of our house required painting by now, so I offered the job to Mike, who willingly accepted.

A few days later I came home to lunch and the phone rang. It was John Price of Gwent Tenting, asking if I knew anyone who would like to work for him in France as a 'camp commandant' for the summer at the camp where our caravan was sited in France.

"I think I know just the man who maybe interested. He's outside up a ladder painting my house, Mike Taylor," I answered.

"I know Mike, he'd be just the type," he replied. I then called Mike from outside and shouted up to him.

"Michael, fancy living and working in France?"

"Anything is better than painting your bloody house!" he answered, jokingly. I told him about the phone call. He came down the ladder and spoke to John and immediately took the job.

He later bought an old Volvo car which I serviced and made good the best we could, and of he went to France for the summer.

We met up several weeks later on our arrival at the camp for our summer holidays with the boys. Jane and Cedric's family followed. What great times we had together.

Mike met a nice French woman by the name of Gislane and they have lived together ever since in France. It just goes to show how a phone call can change one's life.

The following year, 1987, we went down to the caravan to stay. It was also our silver wedding anniversary on August the 18th. Mike and Gislane gave us a surprise party with all the people on the camp invited. It was a lovely gesture and we have remained good friend ever since.

We return nearly every year to visit Mike and Gislane in many parts of France where they have worked and lived and they stay often with us when they visit Wales.

After all the boys had left home, in 1991, Dianne and I moved to a bungalow in Coed-y-Cando Road, about a mile away from Russell Close, near to the railway station north of New Inn.

Sadly, Dianne's sister Jane died in July 1998 with heart rejection failure after a heart transplant a year earlier. Their mother Olwyn died a few months later. My mother passed away in April 1999.

Aunty Marge died on January 2nd 2007 aged 93 in Silverdale.

John Rowland runs a local shop with his wife Janice as he has done for the past forty years.

Some of my time now is also taken up with, at present, six grandchildren.

I also had been a member of Pontnewydd male choir for eleven years until 2006.

Our three boys are all married now. Jonathan had our two oldest grandchildren, James and Emily, while living with former partner, and now lives in Newport with his wife, Debbie, and our youngest grandchild, Lucy.

Richard lives in Penarth, near Cardiff with his wife Helen, and their two children, Megan and Tom.

Martyn has lived in America since 1996 and currently lives in Tampa, Florida, with his wife Jayne and their son Brayden.

Dianne and I celebrated our 45th wedding anniversary in August 2007.

I often sit back in my garden seat, occasionally hearing the sound of steam engines and will always remember being on that platform in 1943, saying goodbye to Aunty Marge all those years ago.

With Dianne and Jonathan, Richard and Martyn

Family Tree

My maternal grandparents

James Henry Jones married **Carrie Rogers**

They had 15 children

Floss married – Evan Price 4 children Colin Audrey Pearl Meryl	**Phyllis** married – Bert Sherman 2 children Malcolm Alan	**Millie** married – Jim Atkinson 3 children Patricia David Philip
Alf married – May Virgin	**Marge** married – George Smith 4 children Jean Michael Esme Mary	**Jack** married – Joan Tew
Ursula married – Aubrey Jenkins 4 children Brian Mary Derek Susan	**Albert** married – Ann Cox 2 children David Alan	**Olwyn** married – Freddie Huggins 2 children Elaine Peter
Dolly married – Dai Virgin 1 child John	**Bill** married – Peggy Davies 3 children Dianne Valerie Kevin	**Kathleen** married – Sid Metcalf 2 children Martin Michael
Gwyneth married – Jack Purchase 3 children Jacqueline Keith Jane	**Derek** married – Mary Knighly 3 children Cledwyn Garry Glynis	**Esme** married – Trevor Pritchard 3 children Jeffrey Philip Karen

Family Tree

My paternal grandparents

George Jenkins married Jane Walters

They had 7 children

Emily married – Eddie Rowlands 2 children Margaret John	**Edward (Ted)** never married	**Aubrey** married – Ursula Jones 4 children Brian Mary Derek Susan
Reece never married	**Joyce** married – Melvin Probert 2 children Mary Angela	**Margaret** married – Frank Beer 2 children David Steven

Iris
married – Derek Hawkins

4 children

Jane
Lyndon
Garry
Mary

Printed in the United Kingdom
by Lightning Source UK Ltd.
127700UK00001B/76-102/P